THE
SEVEN
SECRETS
TO
HEALTHY,
HAPPY
RELATIONSHIPS

Also by don Miguel Ruiz Jr.

The Mastery of Self: A Toltec Guide to Personal Freedom

Living a Life of Awareness:
Daily Meditations on the Toltec Path

The Five Levels of Attachment:
Toltec Wisdom for the Modern World

Don Miguel Ruiz's Little Book of Wisdom:
The Essential Teachings

Also by HeatherAsh Amara

Warrior Goddess Training:
Become the Woman You Are Meant to Be

The Warrior Goddess Way:
Claiming the Woman You Are Destined to Be

Awaken Your Fire: Ignite Your Passion, Find
Your Purpose, and Create the Life That You Love

The Toltec Path of Transformation:
Embracing the Four Elements of Change

THE
SEVEN
SECRETS
TO
HEALTHY,
HAPPY
RELATIONSHIPS

DON MIGUEL RUIZ JR.
& HEATHERASH AMARA

Hierophant publishing

Cover design by Emma Smith
Cover art by Nicholas Wilton
Interior design by Frame25 Productions

Hierophant Publishing
8301 Broadway, Suite 219
San Antonio, TX 78209
888-800-4240
www.hierophantpublishing.com

If you are unable to order this book from your local bookseller,
you may order directly from the publisher.

Library of Congress Control Number: 2018951171

ISBN 978-1-938289-82-8

10 9 8 7 6 5 4 3 2

Printed on acid-free paper in the United States.

To all whom we have loved and who have loved us.

Love is not about property, diamonds and gifts. It is about sharing your very self with the world around you.
—Pablo Neruda

Contents

Introduction

*And will I tell you that these three lived happily
ever after? I will not. . . . but there was happiness.
And they did live.*
—Stephen King

"Happily ever after."

It is with these three little words that an entire
universe of expectations about relationships is created. Through this fairy-tale concept and others like
it, the idea is planted in our minds that once we have
a committed relationship our lives will be grand,
everything will be perfect, and we will have finally
"arrived" at our destination.

But of course we all know relationships are a bit
more complicated than that.

As human beings, most of us yearn for fulfill-
ing relationships, as they are an integral part of
our journey. They provide unlimited ways for us to
learn, grow, thrive, and have fun, as well as serve as
the foundation on which most of us build a family

and community. Yet, as we know, relationships are not always "a bed of roses."

Romantic relationships can take us from sublime ecstasy to the deepest despair with just a word or look from our beloved. They can lift us to great heights of clarity, passion, and openheartedness or drop us suddenly into a pit filled with the fear, grief, confusion, and judgment.

Romantic relationships can prove especially challenging in these changing times. The institution of marriage began as a financial and social arrangement and was not focused on love. Even in our modern times, it was not very long ago that we had distinct gender roles within a relationship. It was idealized that women would stay home and take care of the kids and household while men worked to provide for the family financially. It's easy to see where these roles can fall apart: not only are they inherently stereotypical and unfair, but they were also class discriminatory, since usually only upper-middle-class and upper-class families could afford to have only one parent providing a source of income. Even when both parents had to work, employment opportunities were, and can still be, highly gendered. While these rigid definitions of relationships did not bring happiness, they did bring a kind of familiar stability and continuity.

Today, we are entering a whole new world of relationships—particularly romantic relationships. While we can appreciate the beauty of a vast frontier with no rules, we must also face the challenge of very little guidance or support about how we might behave. For this reason, we usually end up unconsciously dragging the old rules and expectations of our parents, culture, and religion into our relationships—whether or not we consciously agree with them! We choose partners in a flush of hormones and possibility, only to find that when the spark of new love dissipates we have no idea how to communicate or navigate the challenges that arise. And because we are not taught how to be creative, curious artists of relationships, we get bogged down in our expectations and play out the same patterns and conflicts even as the relationships themselves change.

This book arose partly to address this search for knowledge. In our work, we hear many of the same complaints repeated by people seeking guidance about how to find and maintain a healthy relationship. The common issues include everything from "my partner isn't emotionally available" to "I no longer feel physically attracted to my partner" to "I feel like my partner is trying to control me."

Specific questions we have received go something like this:

- How do I communicate my true feelings to my partner about issues we don't agree on?

- How can I come back into trust and love with my partner after an affair or other breach of trust?

- How do I support my partner's path without compromising my own?

- How can I get my partner to grow with me mentally, emotionally, and spiritually?

- How can I feel emotionally close to my partner again?

- How can I help rekindle the sexual chemistry we once had?

- How do I know if it's time to leave the relationship?

- How do I attract a partner who doesn't follow the same patterns in my past?

As you will see in the pages that follow, the answers to these questions lie in healing your past, learning new skills for the present, and envisioning your future clearly. For this we need new guidelines. Our purpose in writing this book is that it can be just such a guide.

Because most of us have been beguiled by some version of the many old fairy tales or myths, such as the elusive happily-ever-after, one of our goals is to help you spot and let go of any personal mythologies that are no longer helpful, thereby opening yourself up to new territories of self-exploration, creativity, and, most importantly, unconditional love.

In our view, unconditional love is the key ingredient of healthy and happy relationships, and the secrets to bringing unconditional love to all your relationships are what we will share with you here. But in order to bring unconditional love to our relationships, we first want to note two key stumbling blocks that keep us from experiencing unconditional love in the first place: domestication and conditional love. To be more specific, unconscious domestications and adherence to the practice of conditional love lead to almost all of the trouble we experience in our relationships. Please allow us to explain.

Much of what we learn about relationships comes to us from our *domestication*, or the system by which we learn society's acceptable modes of behaviors. When it comes to relationships, this means that we learn what we are supposed to gain, how we should behave, and what we are to expect from a multitude of clues, actions, and directives. This includes the ideas we get from movies, songs, and TV, as well as what we witnessed in the behavior of our parents and others as we grew up.

In order to have a truly happy and healthy relationship, we must be willing to examine the ideas that we have been domesticated to, because as you probably know by now, many of those ideas simply do not work. Even the aforementioned "happily ever after" is a simple example of an idea that many of us are domesticated into believing as children. Once we reach adulthood, most of us realize that this particular idea doesn't describe relationships accurately, yet we still cling to it—sometimes subtly or even unconsciously.

Other examples of domesticated ideas around relationships include things such as "I must be who my partner wants me to be" or "I will only be worthy of love and acceptance if I look or behave in a certain way." There are many more of these ideas swirling around us from a very young age.

These domestications result in what we call *conditional love*. To be clear, most people don't call it conditional love; they just call it love. That's how entwined we are with this particular domestication pattern. For instance, do any of the following attitudes sound familiar? You may have heard them from an external source like a partner, but also in your own internal discourse.

- I will love you if . . . you make me feel good about myself.

- I will love you if . . . you make certain promises to me and always keep those promises.

- I will love you if . . . you tell me you love me too.

The corollary to each of these statements, of course, is that if you do not do these things, love will be withheld. You will be alone, unworthy, and defective. In this way, love can take on the characteristics of control and possession in our relationships. That doesn't mean that real love doesn't exist in those relationships simultaneously—it certainly can—but when we place conditions on our love, it will eventually lead to suffering for ourselves and others.

It's also important to point out that not all domestications are bad. Most of us were domesticated to ideas such as "be kind to others," "tell the truth," etc. Part of the groundwork for having a happy and healthy relationship is to notice all your domestications and *see which ones are true for you and which ones are not.*

One easy example is the long-standing idea, with many religious and societal underpinnings, that "couples should get married before having sex." Of course, very few people actually practice this in today's world—they decide that this domestication is not true or useful for them. It's important to note that your mind may continue to believe this domestication, though, even when your heart might not. The result is that you will have sex prior to marriage and likely beat yourself up for it afterward even if you think you are free of this belief. We want to be clear that whether or not you reject or embrace this belief as true in your heart and mind ultimately doesn't matter. What matters is that your rejection or acceptance of this belief is what you truly want, not what you have simply been programmed or indoctrinated to believe.

While conditional love and the underlying domestications can exist across any type of relationship, it's our romantic relationships that often bring out the best and the worst in us. New love emerges almost magically sometimes—filled with possibility and deeply healing. We feel completely seen and cherished, held in the embrace of love. Yet even the best romantic partnerships can become stale and lifeless if they aren't nurtured properly, and the most sublime of these connections can experience a winter of hurt, anger, and conflict over time.

How to Use This Book

We'd like to make clear that we don't call the principles in this book secrets because they are hidden away. In fact, many of them may feel familiar to you and might even be related to concepts that you have already begun to explore. We call them secrets in the sense that they are focal points, ways to orient our understanding and our actions into productive channels that will lead to deeper, more meaningful connections. Part of the secret, as you will see, is in the art of putting these ideas into practice in our lives, day after day and year after year, and realizing when we have veered off course and can decide to return to them again.

After all, relationships don't make themselves or continue happily on autopilot once they begin. If we think of our journey with our beloved as sailing a boat out into the open ocean together, we can understand the layers of complexity involved. If we sit in that boat passively and wait to cruise off into the sunset, we are in for certain disaster. If we throw ourselves into the fullness of the experience—and are willing to do the work that arises—we enter the realm of conscious engagement and connection. It is here that the true journey begins.

The seven secrets to healthy, happy relationships—commitment, freedom, awareness, healing, joy, communication, and release—can help you at any stage in your intimate partnering, whether you've been with someone for many years or are currently single and want to prepare for a partnership.

The first three—commitment, freedom, and awareness—are what we call the foundational secrets. In our view, these are the bedrock upon which all healthy relationships are built. As you read about them, you may notice some areas in your thinking and actions around relationships that need improvement. The good news is that the information contained herein can show you how to repair any faulty foundation you find, replacing old ideas and beliefs with new and stronger beams of support going forward.

The next three—healing, joy, and communication—are all transformative. When you bring the teachings and tools we provide in these chapters into your interactions with others, you can improve and enhance an existing solid union or even rebuild the framework of most damaged structures, transforming them into a clean, spacious, and sturdy way of being.

The last secret—release—provides guidance on nourishing your relationship on an ongoing basis. This is where you learn the skills to perform the maintenance and provide the sustenance that will keep the construction of your relationship solid, including in the midst of changing and challenging times.

While much of what we have to say will focus on romantic relationships, the truth is that these seven principles can help you create deeper and more meaningful connections in *all* of your relationships. As we expand our abilities within relationships, we reap rewards for ourselves. In our experience, investing in the relationships that matter to us most brings powerful opportunities for personal growth.

This will take work and presence and learning new skills. Each of us comes to relationships with a suitcase filled with our history and our hurts, our emotional wounding and our fears. We start by learning to see ourselves as artists, develop the skills to creatively, passionately release what no longer serves us, and craft our unique version of relationships as art.

In this book, we merge the experiences, mistakes, and celebrations of two people well versed in the art of relationships. We are two individuals, but we are choosing to speak with one voice for simplicity and because our teachings are so aligned. Both of us have dedicated our lives to finding our own personal truth and personal freedom, and we agree that relationships are one of the most powerful catalysts for personal growth.

We are also very different. Miguel is happily married to his wife of fifteen years, Susan, and the father of two children, Audrey and Alejandro. Heather-Ash is happily divorced, bisexual, sometimes polyamorous and sometimes monogamous. As we share the stories of people we know, we are also drawing on the breadth and depth of our own experiences with relationships in each chapter, recounting what we've learned through heartbreak and vulnerable loving, through conflict and celebrations.

As we outline the seven secrets to happy and healthy relationships, we will ask you to reevaluate some of the things you have learned about love. To truly absorb these teachings, you must be willing to release old stories from your childhood view of love, along with your blatant or hidden expectations of those you love and your focus on what they should or shouldn't be doing. This focus on what our partner is doing is such a pervasive thought that we are often approached at our workshops and asked something like, "What can I do to get my partner to change their behavior?" While we understand the helpful intention that typically accompanies this type of request, we want to be clear about one thing before we begin: You cannot change anyone else. You can only change yourself. There is no more difficult place to practice this inherent truth than in your most intimate relationships.

If you picked up this book in hopes of finding some magical tool for how to change your partner, you could be disappointed in the pages that follow.

That being said, we invite you to join us on this journey with an open mind, as you may find that changing yourself is all that ever needs to occur for you to be happy.

These pages are full of practical experiences and applications to improve all of your relationships—especially your intimate ones. This includes helping you create an intimate relationship that feeds your heart and soul. We include a section at the end of each chapter with some further explorations you can practice on your own. At the same time, this book is not a traditional how-to manual, because each relationship is as unique as the individuals who form it. There is no one right way to be in relationship, and no strict set of rules will lead to everlasting joy.

Whether you are single, married, celibate, polyamorous, straight, gay, queer, bisexual, or however you choose to identify, we welcome you. Intimacy starts with your relationship with yourself and expands into owning and honoring your choices and desires. There is no one way to travel this path to happy and healthy relationships; there is only *your* way.

In the fairy tales of our childhoods, "happily ever after" was used to signify the end of the story—but for us, and for the guidance in this book, "happily ever after" is only the beginning of a new story: the story of your healthy, happy relationship with yourself and your beloved. Let this be your guide to stepping into the flow of love, with yourself, with your beloved, with your family, and with life.

THE
FOUNDATIONAL
SECRETS

Chapter 1

The Secret of Commitment

*If you have built castles in the air, your work
need not be lost; that is where they should be.
Now put the foundations under them.*
—Henry David Thoreau

Think back to a time when you were a teenager—
when so many of us are our most awkward, vulnerable selves. Our hormones surge into overdrive. We're
bursting with new desires and locked down by old
fears. Will I be seen? Will I be understood? Will I
ever be loved? During this time, we often convince
ourselves that if we could only find a special someone
who will be our partner, all will be right in the world.

In our first forays into relationships, for better
or worse, many of us make a series of commitments
that can set the stage for serious difficulties later on:

- We commit to keeping someone
  special happy.

- We commit to telling our special someone what they want to hear.

- We commit to looking and acting a certain way, all for the benefit of our special someone.

- We commit to being the person we imagine that special someone wants us to be.

Of course, you can see where this is going. Each of these commitments is how we seek approval, attention, and love. But every step we take in this direction moves us farther away from the fundamentals which all human beings require to be happy and healthy: honesty, contentment, self-acceptance, and self-love.

And yet we make these teenage commitments almost universally. And that's okay. They are part of how we grow up and discover ourselves, and they can provide a good jumping-off point as we start our early journeys of self-discovery. The problem is that many of us continue to bring these old ideas and practices into our mature relationships, even when we're in our twenties, thirties, forties, or beyond. If we don't replace those early ideas with another way of doing things and different kinds of commitment, we can find ourselves in real difficulty later on in our relationships.

You may be reading this and thinking, "That's not me, I don't do that." But the habit of altering who you are for someone else can be subtle and hard to break, even for those of us who have been doing inner work for years. Look deeply into yourself. Are there ways in which you look to your special someone, or potential special someone, for clues about who you should be and how you should act?

Domestication, or the ways we are encouraged to behave that society finds acceptable, has played a big role in the development of the idea that we need to commit to changing ourselves to make someone else happy. The media endlessly portrays this type of behavior as normal, necessary, and even advantageous when it comes to finding that special someone, particularly a special someone with whom we would like to share a lifetime commitment. Think of the movie *Jerry Maguire*, in which Tom Cruise as Jerry says, "You complete me."

When he says this, we see the character's underlying belief: if he is complete only through his relationship with his beloved, then he is otherwise essentially incomplete. However, in our view, and in the ancient wisdom of so many others, each of us is *already complete*, right here and right now. In fact, there is nothing else we need to be other than who we are in this moment. The goal of happy and healthy relationships is to form a true partnership where you share the joys and pains of being human.

With that in mind, consider this radical idea regarding commitment: What if that special someone you commit to—no matter what else or who else comes along—is *you*?

The real secret behind commitment in relationships is that it all starts with a commitment to *yourself*. This is foundational, because if we don't honor who we are, it is impossible for us to truly honor another. Most of us, whether we have been in a relationship for twenty years or are currently looking for one, need to learn how to truly, deeply, fully commit to ourselves, no matter what. But what does that really mean? And how do we do that?

Committing to yourself begins with dropping the ideas that you must change in order to be loved by someone else and that you need someone else to be complete. Anytime you are seeking to complete yourself through being accepted by another, you are actually leaving yourself. While this may seem to work in the short term, such as when a relationship is brand-new and everything seems magical, the truth is that you are only kicking the can farther down the road. That is to say, you're putting the problem off rather than dealing with it, which will only cause it to resurface in the future. At some point in our lives, we all must face ourselves directly and learn to embrace what we find.

This commitment to yourself continues by releasing judgment in favor of compassion, letting go of feeling victimized in favor of being honestly vulnerable, and shifting your focus away from who you think others want you to be and toward finding out who you are now.

We'd like to share with you three tools that are foundational when it comes to committing to yourself: breaking up with your judge, breaking up with your victim, and claiming what you want more of in your life.

Breaking Up with Your Judge

Have you ever noticed that unhelpful voice in your mind? It tells you that you aren't good enough and discourages you from trying something new because you might "fail." When it comes to relationships, it's the voice that reminds you of past mistakes and then berates you for making them in the first place. It's your own voice, of course, but this is the part of you that we call the judge.

The judge often comes out when you are fearful, lonely, or regretful or are experiencing any variety of other negative emotions. The judge will also speak up in response to external stimuli, such as when you see a scene in a movie that reminds you of a past relationship "mistake" or you're around someone who reminds you of an ex. In these moments, the judge will rush in to remind you that you "failed."

Statements such as "if only I hadn't divorced/married that person, my life would be better now," or "if my body looked more like his/hers, then I would be happy," are common judgments that many people tell themselves, though these can certainly vary from person to person. Pronouncements such as these are from our judge, and they are never helpful in terms of developing a happy and healthy relationship with ourselves.

What many people don't realize is that how you speak to yourself affects your relationships with others. As an example, consider the following scenarios.

Jan is a busy professional who takes great pride in the work she does for her clients, but when things don't go well at work on a given day, she berates herself for it, often without realizing it. The judge voice in her mind tells her that if her work isn't perfect then it's not worthy—and if her work isn't worthy, then neither is she. This often causes a spiral of similar thoughts, all starting with whatever went wrong at work and ending in attacks and insults against her very self-worth. This self-flagellation darkens her mood considerably, and then she comes home from work to her unsuspecting partner. Because she created so much negativity in herself by listening to her judge, she often snaps at her partner or is in no mood for fun.

When Jan began to notice her internal judge and the effect it was having on her mood, she changed. She committed to supporting herself rather than judging herself. Her partner was the ancillary beneficiary of her improved mood, and it was all the result of her committing to herself first and foremost.

When you listen to and believe your inner judge, you are more likely to judge your partner, too. Imagine this: You and your partner have made a commitment to save toward a goal. Your judge crafts a controlling set of rules about money, praising every penny you pinch and admonishing you for spending on anything that might not be a strict necessity. It sets the tone for the rules to be followed, whether or not you spell them out together. You tell your partner you want them to "quit spending money on frivolous things," and your judge approves this message. After all, you are being clear about your needs and expectations, right? But with this kind of message, sooner or later your judge will be on a collision course with the well-being of your partnership. No one can live up to the demands of your internal judge—not you and not your partner. The judge quickly loses sight of the positive values of your decision together—the warmth of shared goals, the give-and-take of communication—and replaces them with its own "factual" version of events. This is a recipe for resentment.

Our judge is also the resident enforcer of our domesticated ideas of perfection. When it comes to committing to ourselves fully, one of the key pieces that many of us struggle with is feeling unworthy. How can we commit to ourselves when we are so imperfect in so many ways? The judge in us helps to create an image of perfection that we use as a measuring stick against ourselves: "this is how I am" versus "this is how I should be." This split that occurs in our minds leads us to reject or abandon ourselves until we can achieve perfection. We tell ourselves, "if I could only look this way" or "if I can achieve this," only then will we be okay enough with ourselves to accept ourselves.

Because we rarely live up to those "perfect" expectations, we end up rejecting ourselves over and over again. (And even if we do manage to live up to the image of perfection, most of us simply use that occasion to raise the bar even higher.) This starts a vicious cycle, as our self-rejection leads us to fear that we will be rejected by others. We hope somebody else out there will help us feel connected, loved, and complete, but we are also simultaneously terrified that they will reject, abandon, or judge us (because we have already done that to ourselves). In order to mitigate that risk, we commit to changing ourselves into who or what we imagine they want us to be. The problem is that we lose ourselves in the process.

How do we break this cycle? Committing to ourselves starts with accepting and loving ourselves *exactly as we are right now*. It is as simple, and as complex, as that. We let go of who we think we are supposed to be, who we wish we were, and who we think others in our life want us to be. Doing this is the first step in coming home to ourselves.

Commitment to ourselves continues when we make the decision to break up with the judge. This isn't easy to do. For most of us, our relationship with our judge is one of the longest relationships we've been in!

The Importance of Compassion

Breaking up with the judge starts by noticing when it speaks. For so many of us, our inner dialogue is incredibly negative, especially in the area of relationships. We're so tied in with our judge that when they speak (always in our own voice), we mistake the judgments for facts and we punish ourselves accordingly.

Take a look at these statements and notice when you have said something similar to yourself recently:

- "I'm so stupid. I can't believe I did that again!"

- "My legs/hips/thighs/fill-in-the-blank are too fat! I am not lovable."

- "I'm such a failure. I'll never get this right."

These are just a few of the ways that our inner judge speaks, and when it does, we often don't even realize the damage we are doing to ourselves in the process.

Sometimes our judge shows up in disguise, posing as a "helpful friend." For instance, if you aren't paying attention, your judge can sneakily turn any spiritual and self-help practice into a tool for self-flagellation. We judge ourselves for not being compassionate enough, forgiving enough, or self-loving enough. In this way, we can turn any positive principle for transformation into a tool for rejection, with our own judge leading the way.

But here's the thing: this breakup won't be about trying to silence or force the judge to go away, because that self-directed bullying is really just more judging. Using this kind of technique, you would be judging the judge—which is still judging!

The first step to release yourself from the power of your judge is to take a step back, witness your judge's behavior, and have compassion for it rather than condemning it. When you create a little separation between yourself and that negative voice, you can begin to have deep compassion for how you have treated yourself. Instead of listening to the inner hatred, fear, and self-sabotage and accepting them as facts, notice them as judgments. Just noticing them is a step into a new way of being, one based in acceptance, support, and love.

Once you notice your judge, rather than fight it, simply say to yourself, "I'm not going to treat myself like this today. I'm going to love myself instead, including my inner judge." Then remind yourself that you can choose to bring your attention again and again toward the type of relationship with yourself you want to grow—that of your own best friend, one who is completely committed to you. In this way, you will be using the judgments that arise as a cue on when and where to redirect your attention to love. This won't be silencing the judge; the judge will still appear, but each time it does, you will notice what it says with compassion and choose instead to turn away from judgment and focus on love.

Remember: changing your inner relationship with yourself takes time. As you start to notice the moments in which you're not speaking kindly to yourself, do your best to ask, "What would I say to my best friend, or someone I love dearly, if they were in this exact situation?" We will tackle some of these judgments again in a later chapter on healing, but for now simply notice them and begin the breakup process by choosing to love and encourage yourself.

Breaking up with our judge allows us to shift our relationship with our most negative inner critic. When we move on from rejecting and berating ourselves, we finally have the opportunity to listen to the voice of our true needs and desires. But before we can move on to claiming what we really want, there's something else we still need to do: break up with our inner victim.

Breaking Up with Your Victim

Now that you've found your judge, it's time to locate your victim. Don't think you have a victim? Well, the truth is that you can't have a judge without a victim, and you can't have a victim without a judge; they are two sides of the same coin. While the judge is that critical voice that says things like "you're not good enough" or "you'll never be loved," the victim is the part of you that listens, believes, and feels bad as a result. It takes the blame and the beating without standing up for itself. Breaking up with your victim starts by questioning the rambling pronouncements of your judge rather than believing them without question.

The good news is that any work you do to break up with one will help as you work toward breaking up with the other. In addition to noticing when your inner victim accepts what your judge is saying without question, you might also become aware of any long-running stories of victimhood that you have adopted. One common story, for instance, goes like this: "If only this or that hadn't happened, my life would be so much better now." The victim believes this story so thoroughly that it no longer seems to be a judgment at all, but merely fact.

Past regrets are one of the biggest sources of fuel for our victim nature. As we work to limit the influence of our victim, it's a good practice to call to mind any past events or decisions you made that you now regret. The process of reframing these "bad" moments can be very helpful in releasing your victim and committing to yourself.

Choose one experience you'd like to reframe, and think of all the reasons why that choice or event was somehow good for you. Please note that this can be a very difficult practice if you've been through an abusive situation, but the point here is to reclaim your power by remembering that good things have come to you, even as a result of painful experiences.

For instance, if you have experienced divorce, your reframed list might include things such as "I learned that I can rely on myself, that I have my own back."

Another trait of the victim is when we shun responsibility, acting as if we have no role in a situation and placing the blame on others instead. However, part of the beauty of committing to you is that you get to take a piece of responsibility for everything that happens in your life. You might balk at this idea, but when you accept responsibility, you reclaim your power by realizing that at the very least you have a choice in how you respond to life's situations.

We may not choose our circumstances, but we can always choose how we respond to them. This is especially true in relationships, in which so many of us tend to play the victim of a partner who isn't living up to our expectations (especially when we think we have done so much for them!). This is an example of those old teenage commitments we discussed previously; our tendencies even as adults to try to change for other people—to be, say, or look as we imagine they want us to. When our partners don't respond in kind by trying to also change themselves, then they aren't playing along! When they behave in a way we disapprove of, we say they aren't even trying. They aren't trying to change who they are the way we are changing who we are. We get mad and play the victim: *"How could they do this to me? I have done so much for them!"* So many of us have done some version of this strange dance in our relationships. But we don't have to continue in this way any longer.

When you commit to yourself, you realize that you are responsible for your happiness, and others are responsible for their own happiness. Certainly, it's fine to be considerate and want to do things for the ones we love, but the moment we attach a demand for in-kind behavior, we are no longer loving from our heart, but loving with conditions instead.

Committing to Yourself

While breaking up with your judge involves bringing a quiet, loving, and nurturing attitude to that part of yourself, breaking up with your victim often requires a different energy. Here is where you have to put your grown-up pants on and take responsibility for the events in your life. Committing to yourself places the responsibility on your own shoulders. This doesn't excuse the inappropriate behavior of others, but it does acknowledge that we have a choice in how we respond to any such behavior.

For many people, this is simultaneously freeing and frightening.

We have a mutual friend who, many years ago, was in a relationship with someone who could be physically abusive. Eventually our friend went to see a therapist, who in their very first meeting asked, "So you must like it when he hits you?" Our friend was incensed. "Of course I don't like that! Why would you say that?" she asked. The therapist looked at her square in the eye and replied, "Because you are still in the relationship."

This shook our friend to her core, and she realized that a portion of what the therapist said was true. She would have to undertake the bold step of facing her own willingness to be a victim. While every relationship is unique, for our friend this statement served as a wake-up call that prompted her to free herself from the relationship.

More commonly, a lot of subtle victimization occurs when we wish our partners were different than how they actually are. "If he only liked this . . ." "If she would just think about that . . ." Each of these statements represents one of the little ways in which we give our power away. If we give up this victim mentality, we regain the power to choose how we respond rather than to automatically suffer. We also honor the intrinsic value of our partner—not as a fantasy version of who we think they ought to be, but as a real and whole human being in their own right.

Sometimes your internal judge can be so fast with its pronouncements that you miss them. Or these judgments have been there so long that you believe them—you have made them a part of who you are without even realizing it. When you catch yourself feeling sad, irritable, or anxious, check and see if you are playing the role of victim in some area. If you hear your inner voice wailing, "Why did this happen?" or "This shouldn't have happened!" Or, most of all, the dreaded, "This always happens to *me* . . ." Stop. Listen. Make space. Back up. Call it out. Victims take things personally; that is how they are created. Remember, we all have a choice, and the choice is how we react. Nothing anyone says or does is because of you. When it comes to the bad behavior of others, remember that you're just standing in the target zone. You are collateral damage in their war with themselves.

Once you identify and start to work with your judge and your victim, it's amazing how your relationships with others will also change. Throughout this book, we will explore the many benefits that come to us when we start looking at the good side of things and investing in responses from a place that is neither judge nor victim. Most importantly, the decision to commit to you—to embrace this first relationship secret—means you are taking responsibility for your side of the street, from your nose to your toes, and nothing more.

Claiming What You Want More of in Your Life

As you begin to break up with your judge and your victim, this frees you to answer the foundational question at the center of your commitment to yourself: *What do I want more of in my life?*

When you first ask yourself what you want more of, you might notice that your mind comes up with all sorts of answers. You may be longing for the person you're in a relationship with now to behave in a particular way. Or if you're not in a relationship right now, perhaps you have a mental list of what you want in a future partner.

However, in this moment we'd like you to focus on what you want in a slightly different way. Rather than focusing on people, places, and things, try exploring the feelings that you want to create in your life. For instance, do you want to experience more love in your life? Peace? Compassion? Excitement? Generosity? Communion? Gratitude? Self-acceptance? While the "things" you want will always and forever be changing, the feelings you want to create in your life rarely change.

In all our years of teaching, very few (if any) people have expressed that they would like to feel more fear, guilt, shame, and resentment in their lives. Yet those are exactly the feelings your judge and your victim create within you. More than ever, when we focus on feelings we see the importance of breaking up with our judge and our victim.

Taking Action

Once you have identified the feelings you want to feel, ask yourself what action steps you can take to bring more of these desired feelings into your life. This is where things get fun. This is the time to tap into your creative energy and awaken your inner sense of wonder and play.

For example, if you're craving more love, how do you bring that sense of love into your life? A good starting place is to close your eyes and think of someone or something—it could be a child or a pet—that is easy to love. Someone who, when you think of them, lightens and brightens your heart. Luxuriate in that feeling for a little while. Feel the warmth of love and notice the sensations in your body. Then see if you can extend that same kind of joyful love to yourself. From this place, you can let your mind explore and come up with ways to bring more of that sense of love into your life. You might try making a beautiful meal for yourself, walking in nature, or spending time pampering yourself.

Here's the bonus: as you arrange to take actions that bring yourself love, you begin to understand more about what it is you really want deep in your heart, through the physical experience and emotional feeling of those wants. Then you will be so much better equipped to reach out and ask for what you want from other people. You have to start by nourishing yourself first, by taking responsibility for feeding yourself the love, compassion, and gentleness you crave. This will allow you to be more intimate, present, and playful with others.

As you fill up your inner reserves of the love, peace, and generosity that you deeply desire, you will find that all of your relationships will shift. You are no longer trying to get approval from the outside or resenting a perceived lack of what you need. This allows you to rest into being the best you can be and releases your actions so that they can come from your love, rather than from your judgment or victimhood. Embrace this radical, beautiful transformation as you find you can be at peace with the person you are right now. From this place, you can be sure that any desire to create change in your behavior and circumstances will come from the love and support of yourself, rather than from a place of criticism and fear.

Committing to Another

Committing to ourselves provides a firm foundation from which we can commit to others in a real way. Commitment to self should never be thought of as a path to be completely independent or a way to pretend we don't need anyone else. The truth is, we are all interdependent. Any notion that we can be absolutely independent is often based in ego. We must continue to find a balance between filling ourselves up, finding love within, and recognizing we are tribal, community-minded creatures who need friendship, affection, and love.

Others in our lives are precious gifts, and we enjoy and honor those gifts most wholly when we are centered and grounded in ourselves. In this way, committing in a relationship is about making a choice to say yes to another human with a whole and open heart.

Deeply grounded in our love for ourselves, we can begin to think about what types of commitments we are making to others. Here are some foundational commitments we can make in our relationships:

- ◆ To show up.

- ◆ To be present.

- ◆ To listen.

- ◆ To be open-minded.

- ◆ To be willing to grow.

- ◆ To be kind.

- ◆ To be loving.

- ◆ To do our best.

- ◆ To help each other with mutual respect.

Beyond these, again, we get to turn on our imaginative brain and tap into our true desires. We get to do the difficult and rewarding work of finding out what we really want and what we are willing to commit to within a happy and healthy relationship.

Just as every person is one of a kind, so too is every relationship unique. Some people may be willing to commit to things that others will not, and that's okay. What's important is that you are honest and able to communicate what works for you and what does not. (We'll cover how to communicate this effectively in chapter six.)

Once you have solid inner commitment with yourself, then you expand out and focus on each individual relationship in your life. The first secret to a happy, healthy relationship starts with you and your commitment to yourself: to embrace yourself, to break up with your judge and victim, and to decide what you want. From this place, this clean mirror, you can commit to someone else in the capacity you both agree to, with clear eyes and open hearts.

Explorations

Commitment to Self-Intention

Rituals, prayers, and mantras can help us solidify what we want to manifest in our lives. They act as an outward expression of an inner desire; in this case your desire to affirm your commitment to yourself.

Put one hand over your heart and one on your belly. Take a breath and bring your intention inward, into yourself.

Say the following out loud:

> *I commit to bringing a new relationship with myself into being. I commit to learning how to love myself in this moment and this time, as I am. I commit to being compassionate and gentle and fiercely loving with myself. I commit to getting to know the being I am right now. I commit to no longer abandoning or rejecting myself; I commit to staying with myself on this journey of life at my pace and in my own time.*

Speaking this out loud to yourself voices your inner commitment to yourself. That's your first step to consciously committing to yourself, and you will bring this dedication along into your relationship with others. You are stepping into this journey of life as a friend and ally to yourself.

Feeling Visualization

Let's do a feeling-based visualization to step into this way of relating to ourselves.

Make a list of the feelings you want to experience more of. For example, you might want more peace, compassion, love, excitement, joy, generosity, ease, communion, gratitude, or self-acceptance.

After you've listed a few of the feelings you want to create more of, the next step is to experience those feelings in the body. Close your eyes and take a breath into your belly. What feeling do you want to experience more of? Imagine giving yourself the gift of that feeling. Think of a person or thing that makes you feel love, and let that feeling generate inside you. Notice the physical sensations of the love you are experiencing. How does it feel in your belly? Does it have a temperature? A vibration? A sound?

Do the same for gratitude. What are you grateful for? Can you feel that gratitude in your mind and body?

How does peace feel? Visualize yourself on a beach, on a mountaintop, in a forest, or wherever your peaceful place is. Experience the feelings of deep peace.

Stay in this practice for at least fifteen minutes, and when you have run through all the emotions on your list, thank yourself for being open and present in this exercise.

This practice can be used to access and attract any emotion into your life and is a great place to start to get ideas on how to bring more of these feelings into your life on a daily basis.

Making Time for You

Forming new habits is one of the most powerful practices available to us. It can help break down bigger wants into smaller pieces that we can integrate into our daily routines. If you want to make more time for a loving relationship with yourself, start small.

Decide that each day you will make one small gesture that opens up a little time for you. Commit to making a cup of tea for yourself. Pick a movie and put it in your calendar as an official date with yourself. Take a walk without your phone. It can even be as simple as committing to one moment per day of looking in the mirror and saying as you would to a dear friend, in the wise words of Fred Rogers,

"Remember, I like you just for being you." Commit to one of these small gestures per day, and see where it leads you. We think you'll want to do more.

Chapter 2

The Secret of Freedom

I said "until death do us part—
not breakfast, lunch, and dinner."
—Unknown

The next foundational secret to happy and healthy relationships is freedom, as so many of our domesticated ideas of love are tied to a lack of it. We can see it in our metaphors for committed relationships: we speak of the "bonds" of marriage or the "old ball and chain," or we hear that someone is finally "tied down." The truth is that while constant physical proximity might be desired and attainable in the first flush of a new love, as a relationship matures and grows freedom becomes more and more necessary.

As we build on the first foundational secret—that of commitment to ourselves—we now embrace the seeming paradox that only by extending real freedom to our beloved can we open the door to deeper, more meaningful connection. Furthermore, like a boomerang, the freedom we proffer comes right back to us. When we free others, we also free ourselves.

Relationships thrive when both partners feel free and when there is room to grow and stretch in new and fascinating ways. In a partnership like this, each person shares responsibility for the relationship as an entity in and of itself—the sea stretched between shores, which is wild and unknowable and yet also defined by and confined within the lands that border it. Freedom in a relationship means that both parties are responsible for their own well-being yet each chooses to share this fascinating journey of life together. Each party continuously makes conscious choices, free of domesticated ideas and societal influences.

Some of you reading this may be thinking, "But I don't feel this type of freedom and spaciousness in my current relationship." That's understandable, given the number of messages, subtle and overt, that bombard us in our society. And it's okay. Remember, freedom is an ongoing, evolving negotiation of give-and-take. Where you are today does not have to dictate where you will arrive tomorrow. The good news is that there are some specific steps you can take to foster an atmosphere of freedom. But before we get to those, let's look at some of the behaviors that can stifle and suffocate the feeling of freedom between couples.

Attempts to Control

Many of us believe that in order to get what we want in a relationship, we need to coax our partners into behaving how we think they should. We usually accomplish this by offering some type of reward for the desired behavior, typically our love and affection. On the other side of the same coin, we may punish our partners for not behaving the way we want them to. We might berate them in emotional outbursts or subject them to passive-aggressive behavior such as withholding our love and affection.

In these ways, we make our love conditional in an attempt to domesticate our partners into doing what we want them to do, instead of encouraging them to follow their heart and be who they are in the warmth and strength of our unconditional love.

Here's a simple example of this in action. Joe and Mary have been in a long-term committed relationship for many years. Although they have plans for a dinner at Joe's parents' house, Mary calls him that morning and tells him that some friends have an extra ticket to an event that night, and she asks Joe if it would be okay if she attended that instead of the dinner. Joe really wants Mary to come to the dinner, but instead of saying so, he tells her to go with her friends. Joe is secretly upset the rest of the day, and when Mary gets home that night after the event, he is cold and withholds his affection and attention. Mary senses this distance and becomes resentful, choosing to withhold her love as well in retaliation for his punishment of her free choice.

If Joe and Mary had managed to communicate better, this issue might have been averted. We will certainly be exploring communication in great detail in chapter six because good communication practices are vital to happy and healthy relationships. But for now, our focus is on the motives and the energy created between the partners in this situation.

In this instance, not only is Joe punishing Mary by withholding love (as well as punishing himself), he is also letting Mary know that if she behaves this way in the future, she can expect more of the same. He is trying to influence and control her future behavior. Mary is sending a similar message—that punishment she deems unjust will be met with more punishment, rather than curiosity, understanding, or love. In this way, both parties are trying to domesticate each other to their respective points of view. As a result, the night might explode into an argument, or they might both go to bed carrying these negative emotions with them. As you can imagine, neither of these options are conducive to happiness.

It's all so obvious from the outside. Most of us can spot this type of passive-aggressive and controlling behavior in others, but we have much more difficulty identifying it in our own behavior. We tend to be very attached to whatever beliefs compel us to act in these ways. This is especially true when we justify our actions by telling ourselves that we have our partner's best interest at heart or that we are trying to get them to behave in a certain way "for their own good." In fact, we have been conditioned to believe that this kind of caring for others is part of the central definition of what love *is*.

The truth is that we don't know what is best for anyone else, even when we have their best interests at heart. Everyone else, including your beloved, is on their own path. We really don't know what is best for them, even when we think we do. Only by extending freedom can we truly allow—and trust—our partner to figure out what is best for them.

Admittedly, it's easy to allow someone the freedom to be who they are when they are doing things we like. The challenge is to extend this same spirit of freedom when they are doing things we don't like. For instance, can we extend freedom to a partner who is late (again)? Who has differing political views? Who refuses to engage or communicate with us about certain topics? Who has different views on parenting (either in relation to kids you share or kids from prior relationships)? Life generously gives us plenty of times to practice allowing others the freedom to be who they are.

Unconditional love says, "I choose to respect your freedom to make your choices and decisions, even if I don't like them." Conditional love says, "I will grant you freedom to make your own choices and decisions as long as they serve me and my agenda in some way." The former is true freedom; the later is control.

One of the things that makes the desire to control others such a difficult habit to break is that sometimes it appears to work. We either coax or force our will on someone and they comply, so our ego takes the bait. When our will works out well for both parties, we declare victory. You might be aware of this type of victory when you hear yourself say, "I told you so!" to your partner. This is a very typical victory cry in this area, because it celebrates how what we deemed helpful to someone else turned out to be true—even though we may make them feel hurt in the long run by instilling our will on them rather than letting them decide for themselves (even if their decision proves to be a mistake). The truth is that you can't control anyone else's behavior for very long, as everyone is responsible for their own choices and actions in all circumstances—including you. Even when it seems to work, it's only a matter of time (sometimes a long time) before the other person rebels, but eventually they will, in one form or another.

Sometimes our efforts at control arise from different motives. For instance, if we have been hurt in the past, we may consciously or unconsciously feel the need to protect ourselves. In this instance, we might use conditional love to try to stay safe by keeping others in line so they won't have a chance to hurt us. However, this behavior is really just another way we close our hearts off at the deepest level. We attempt to buffer ourselves from being hurt, not realizing that our attempts to play it safe through control will actually cause more pain in the long run. When we shield ourselves from pain by shutting down ourselves or others, we also block expressions of joy and the free-flowing energies of love.

Human beings have an innate desire to be free. If we don't extend that sense of freedom to those we are in a relationship with, ultimately they will want to change the terms of the relationship or leave it altogether, even if they aren't conscious that their desire to be free is the reason. When one person controls another for long enough, the resistance swells until there is a breakout, and it usually isn't pretty. Either the controlled person openly revolts, or they do something behind the back of the controller, typically leaving the controller surprised.

Anytime we attempt to control someone—whether it's to protect ourselves or to get what we think we want—we open the door to a host of other unwanted and unhelpful outcomes. Whenever we are trying to control something, we are simultaneously closing down our capacity to listen, to learn something new about them, and to adjust to the truth of the present moment. Trying to control also shuts us off from the gifts of our own compassion, dims our creative responses to challenges, and dampens our access to our intuition and inner wisdom.

The case for extending freedom to your partner is a strong one, and now let's look at three simple but very effective ways to create the space for freedom to emerge: encourage your partner to choose what they really want, recognize your partner's accomplishments, and support them in activities that don't involve you.

Encourage Your Partner to Choose What They Really Want

One of the most important ways you can engender freedom in a relationship is to encourage your partner to do what they really want to do in any given situation, rather than asking them to do what you may want them to do. You can start simple here. For instance, "do you want to attend a movie with me, or would you rather go out with your friends?" "Do you feel like eating Chinese food or something else?" Encourage your partner to be open with you about their wants—and remind them that while you might not always like or agree with what they say or do, one of your most important values in a relationship is freedom. In this way, you're conveying to them that your interest in knowing and supporting their deepest desires is a natural extension of your unconditional love for them.

This is not always easy to do with more serious issues, and it is certainly fine to express your own preferences to your partner when appropriate. Just remember that their truth may be different from yours—and that's a good thing. Encouraging them to follow their own heart is a great gift to yourself in that you get to know your partner on a deeper level, because now you are seeing what they really choose in a given situation. Additionally, encouraging your partner to choose what they really want is a concrete way to eliminate the cycle of "you change yourself for me and I'll change myself for you." That cycle always leads to frustration, resentment, and a feeling of constriction in the relationship.

Recognize Your Partner's Accomplishments

Most of us are in tune with the importance of supporting our partner through difficult times such as job loss, health issues, and the like. Doing so is a vital part of a healthy relationship. Sometimes we overlook another powerful means of support, which is applauding your partner when they achieve a goal, take on a new challenge, or otherwise accomplish something meaningful to them. Be mindful that this recognition doesn't spill over into conditional praise, or trying to influence or control your partner's behavior. This type of encouragement—given honestly—helps create an atmosphere of freedom as well as support. "Congrats on getting that promotion," or "I'm so proud of you for trying something new." Your partner feels your enthusiasm for their passionate pursuits and your regard for their accomplishments.

An extension of this is the incorporation of a shared gratitude practice focused on your most intimate relationships. The benefits of gratitude are well documented, as numerous studies have shown that expressing it regularly can improve not just your physical and mental health but also your outlook for the future, and it can even help us sleep better. Expressing your gratitude and thanks to your partner directly is an essential component of a healthy and happy relationship. It also helps create an atmosphere of freedom when we openly acknowledge that which is done or given in a spirit of generosity. The little things are often the most transformative: saying thanks for taking out the trash or picking up the dry cleaning. And certainly the more broad gratitude is welcome, such as a general thanks for being such a great parent. We've included a very effective exercise for enriching your gratitude practice within your relationship at the end of this chapter.

Support Activities That Don't Involve You

We've all heard the cliché about absence making the heart grow fonder, but it points to a deep truth: oftentimes we gain renewed appreciation for what we have by stepping away from it and returning with fresh eyes. One way to help your partner feel freedom in your relationship is to encourage them to engage in pursuits on their own or with other friends—to literally spend some time and energy away from you in a healthy way.

One common lament that we hear in relationships is that one partner is feeling neglected, while the other is feeling constricted. We would venture to say that this is a function of domestication at work: feeling like we aren't "good enough" can lead to trying to boost our value based on another's desire to spend time with us. So we turn to conditioning to try to coax or persuade someone into giving us more closeness. Needless to say, this is not enjoyable for either party and only serves to reinforce the feelings of inadequacy. Further, it sets up a no-win situation for the person who is feeling constricted. Either they choose to disappoint their partner by maintaining distance or acquiesce to a demand for attention and resent their choice in the matter.

Relationships facing this difficulty actually benefit most from a renewed commitment to freedom for both parties. The irony is that when you begin to encourage your partner to be free, they often want to spend more time around you. And even if they don't, when you embrace your commitment to loving yourself, you can begin to enjoy your own freedom as well, and love them for being able to do what they want to do. You can even affirm this joy and tell them honestly how exciting it is to watch them thrive and do what they want to do.

Of course, this process may reveal that you both have some work to do in evaluating the agreements you have in the relationship. You can only do this from a place of mutual respect and freedom. Only then can you decide where you want the relationship to go.

These three practices each stand as a powerful tool to make space for more freedom, and when woven together, they can empower a huge shift in your relationships.

Extending Freedom and Making Boundaries

As we mentioned earlier in the chapter, when we allow others freedom, life will offer situations in which our partners choose things we don't like or agree with. What then? How can we hold space for their freedom even when they are acting in ways that we find objectionable? One way to start is by listening to what else is true for us in the situation and turning our focus inward. When we put less of our attention on what our partner is doing and more attention on why those actions make us uncomfortable, we can start to unravel the things within us that make us want to control others. We can acknowledge if we are afraid, scared of, or confused by the choices they are making or contemplating and look deeper inside ourselves for the reason why. We can listen to and support ourselves so that we can be comfortable in these situations while continuing to allow space for our partner's freedom. When you find yourself wanting to change your partner in some way, ask yourself these questions: What am I trying to control? What do I need to let go of?

Allowing another person the freedom to be who they are does *not* mean that you must agree with or like everything that they say or do. We can allow freedom and wish the results of that freedom weren't happening, or not like it, but what is important is to practice choosing what works in the long run rather than achieve a hollow victory by forcing our will on someone. Conditional love and attempting to domesticate others are a deeply ingrained habit and won't be something you stop doing completely right away. The trick is to notice when you are doing this and make a different choice.

To be clear, we are not saying that you should stop making boundaries or that you should simply tolerate someone else's behavior, especially when it's abusive. Remember the bedrock of committing to yourself first? Your freedom is just as important as another's. You must know what you are willing to commit to in a relationship and what you will not allow. After all, your job is to be true to yourself. The other person's job is to be true to himself or herself. When both parties do this, you have laid the groundwork for true freedom, and you can encourage an atmosphere of freedom in a relationship, even with healthy boundaries.

One of the simplest definitions of boundaries we know is from researcher Brené Brown, who says that boundaries are simply what's okay and what's not okay. Just because you are allowing someone freedom doesn't mean you are abandoning your boundaries. The two are not mutually exclusive. Remember that first and foremost, your commitment is to yourself, and creating healthy boundaries—as well as expressing them to those around you—is another way to honor that commitment.

In our view, one way to express a boundary is through a conscious "no." When we look within ourselves and say to another person, "no, I don't want to do that," or "no, that won't work for me," we are speaking with the authority of a conscious no. This "no" reflects your focus on what is true for *you*—what is okay and what's not okay from your perspective. In this process, you must remove any guesses or wishes about what may or may not be true for your partner. In this way, you are committing to you while simultaneously granting freedom to your partner. You are not judging their behavior, guessing at their motivations, or demanding that they change (even if inside you might hope that they do).

Sometimes this can be emotionally difficult, as in the following example. We have a friend whose spouse, after several years of marriage, conveyed to her that he wanted to change their agreement from a monogamous relationship to a sexually open one. She did not share this view and explained that while she loved him and wanted him to be happy, that was a deal breaker for her. She told him that she appreciated his honesty, and now she had to share hers. In this case, she said to him, "You are free to take that route, but please know that I won't be able to stay in this relationship with you if you do." There was no energy of threat or punishment in her response to him; she was simply stating what was true for her. She wasn't making her love conditional; she was simply maintaining her commitment to herself while allowing him the freedom to make his own choices (in contrast to giving him a condition to try and control his choices).

Making a good boundary means that we say "no" clearly and with an open heart, which in most cases involves the willingness to speak up and state your truth. We know that for many people, speaking your truth can be difficult—particularly in the midst of a wrenching emotional moment or a conflict situation. While we will dive into communication later, for now, in the context of our lesson on freedom, we are simply asking that you *become willing* to speak up and state your truth.

Many of us haven't been taught how to make good boundaries without feeling guilty or using them as a way to manipulate another. As a result, you may either apologize profusely for saying no or say no while simultaneously acting out in a passive-aggressive manner, hoping that "if they love you" they will change their own behavior.

In addition, our domestications encourage us to say yes, even when we really mean no, and the result is that we often don't make the boundaries that we need to stay committed to ourselves. If this behavior continues, over time we stifle ourselves, building a dam to hold back our silenced nos. Eventually they form a tidal wave of emotion so powerful that when we finally say no, it comes out as a you-shall-not-pass, over-the-top, emotionally charged outburst rather than a clear and honest boundary.

Remember that setting boundaries with an open heart takes practice, and remind yourself that you are learning. You won't be able to do this perfectly; many of us haven't had good role models for how to create honest, healthy boundaries in the context of freedom, so in many ways we have to make it up as we go along and create role models for ourselves by modeling the behaviors we wish to see on our own.

Every time you say no to someone else you are also saying yes to yourself. Eventually you'll find that there is no difference between sharing or receiving a yes or a no; they are both simply responses that you can give or receive openheartedly. It doesn't mean that you want to say no necessarily, because you love your partner and want them to be happy; it just means that you realize you can't say yes and stay true to yourself. Your response may look something like, "I wish I could say yes to this, because I know it's important to you, but for me it's a no."

When you become good at this practice, a profound change takes place. You'll notice that you stop changing your own behavior based on what you think your partner's reaction will be. You want harmony, but you also know that this isn't possible in all areas. Furthermore, you realize that life without conflict would be very boring! Our disagreements actually help our relationships grow and stay fluid. Through the constant negotiation of different priorities and preferences, we can continue to look at our own beliefs and ideas and see if they have changed, while allowing our partner the space to change if they wish, remembering that their behavior isn't up to us. When you don't need your partner to be different, you can stay present in your disagreements with them, including their upset or fear, without betraying your truth. If you allow them the freedom to feel their own fear, then there's a space for them to find a new way. In moments of difficulty, the more we come back to ourselves, honor our fear, and love ourselves with the intent of extending freedom, the more beautiful, surprising, and authentic the results. Our hearts can learn to stay open even in challenging situations.

Explorations
Shared Context and Differentiation

In his book *Passionate Marriage*, therapist and author David Schnarch suggests that the most bonded intimate relationships happen when couples have what he calls shared context and differentiation. One way to think about this is your shared yeses and your divergent nos in a relationship.

Shared context is your joint yes: the things you and your partner like to do together. Take a moment and examine: Where are your yeses as a couple? What inspires and opens both of you? It might be going to the movies, salsa dancing, or going for long hikes. To build your intimacy and joy with each other, make a plan to do one more thing this week that brings both of you happiness.

The key to locating your shared context is that you have to be honest. If you pretend to like something your partner likes just to "keep the peace," then eventually you will become resentful. Doing something you dislike for your partner's sake every once in a while is fine; there is a beautiful joy in seeing our partner enjoy something, even if we are not thrilled about it. But if you have made a habit of watching football or going to modern art museums or hanging out at the beach when that is not your thing, then you will need to course correct and find out where your true shared context is.

Differentiation is just as valuable as shared context, and in fact it is just as crucial for all committed relationships. We need to have places where we honor our unique passions, separate from our partner. This helps us learn how to honor and share our nos with each other: No, I don't want to go ice-skating, but I'm so happy to drop you off while I go read at the library. No, I'm not interested in watching the soccer game, but I'll make snacks for you and your friends and go for a long walk in the woods. No, I don't want to have children, but I'm open to fostering some older kids. These are divergent nos.

As we open to each other's differences, we get the opportunity to learn about how other people view the world. When we bring respect and curiosity, we learn it's okay to both love and enjoy the places where we have similarities and also love the differences. Recognize that no relationship will be in alignment 100 percent of the time. If you are always in agreement, it probably means that one or the other of you is not saying what is true in order to keep the peace.

Celebrate and open to both your yeses and your nos with each other, and you'll find more peace in your relationship and more fun!

Notice the interactions in the upcoming week where you and your partner have shared contexts (yeses) and differentiation (nos). Do you ever find you or your partner "keeping the peace" to have shared context? Notice if there is a time when encouraging differentiation could provoke a deeper, more honest discussion.

Opening to Yes, Opening to No

At our workshops, we do an exercise early on that helps couples understand the practical implementation of allowing freedom for another as well as yourself. We call it the Yes/No Game.

Yes is a word that conveys freedom. Just think how much better you feel when you say "yes." Now imagine standing across from your beloved (real or imagined) and the feeling of you both saying "yes!" out loud to each other for no specific reason. Feel your enthusiasm, your full-bodied YES being received and mirrored back by your partner's full-body YES.

Now think of the things you agree about. In what moments do you say yes to each other? Yes, we choose to be with each other. Yes, we agree to live in this city. Yes, we want our children to be homeschooled. Imagine the places you say yes with one another, and feel those yeses as they move through your body.

That feels delicious, doesn't it? We all love that feeling of agreement, when our yes is mutual.

Now imagine both you and your partner saying "no" with each other. You both are in agreement with your clear NO. It feels powerful and unified.

You are aligned in your no: No, we are not going to give six hundred dollars to a distant cousin for the fifth time. No, we are not going to allow our neighbors to tear down our back fence. No, we are not going to let the doctor give our child that particular medicine. NO.

Clarity and connection, in both our yes and our no, create a sense of harmony.

And now comes the hard part.

Think of a time when you recently wanted something—you had a full-on YES—but your partner had an equally adamant NO. Or maybe your partner wanted something, but your answer was an absolute NO. How did you resolve it?

Now imagine a new scenario where you and your partner are in disagreement. This is where the work in freedom comes in. This is where it becomes important to try this exercise—with your beloved if they are in agreement—so that you can learn to feel what it is like to be in disagreement, even passionate disagreement.

As you try this exercise, you will become more practiced in holding space for disagreement without letting it lead you into believing that to disagree means that you're going to fight or argue or dissolve your relationship. Disagreement is a part of healthy relationships—what can be unhealthy is how we react to it or when we try to change ourselves or our boundaries to avoid it; so practicing at being in compassionate disagreement can make it more comfortable when disagreement arises naturally.

Gratitude Practice

Here is a simple and powerful practice you can do with your beloved. Every night before you go to sleep, tell your partner three things they did that day that you are grateful for. These things can be little or big, but it helps to be specific. For instance, "I am grateful that you met me for lunch today," or "I am grateful that you listened to me when I was having a bad day at work," or "I am grateful that you picked up the groceries." Invite your partner to do the same. These specific expressions of gratitude not only create a sense of happiness and well-being, they also support an atmosphere of freedom.

Chapter 3

The Secret of Awareness

Awareness is not the same as thought. It lies beyond thinking, although it makes use of thinking, honoring its value and its power. Awareness is more like a vessel which can hold and contain our thinking, helping us to see and know our thoughts as thoughts rather than getting caught up in them as reality.

—Jon Kabat-Zinn

The final secret in the foundational triad of health and happy relationships is awareness. In fact, practicing this secret is necessary for the remaining secrets to unfold and develop, as you can only change something once you become aware of it. For those of you familiar with our other books, you already know that the practice of awareness is one the cornerstones of our work. But for those of you who aren't familiar with this tool, let us start by explaining exactly what we mean by awareness in the context of this book.

On one level, awareness is the art of being fully present, acutely cognizant of what is happening in *this* moment, both within and without. In other words, awareness is the practice of simultaneously observing what is happening in the exterior world while also witnessing our inner reaction to it.

We use the term *awareness* here to describe multiple levels from which you can look within and get to know who you really are, both on your own and through your relationship with another. This work includes everything from expanding your conscious understanding of your likes and dislikes to gaining a deeper knowledge of your strengths, weaknesses, domestications, fears, wounds, and deal breakers. Until you know these things about yourself, it is very difficult to form a deep partnership with someone else.

Those of us who have spent years trying to please others or change ourselves to become what we think others want may be out of touch with our own likes and dislikes on a very basic level. When this happens, we might end up agreeing with, or even advocating for, something in a relationship that is inconsistent with our inner truth. The disconnect between our true desires and our domesticated ideals very often leads to profound confusion and unhappiness.

Additionally, we all have relative gifts and short-comings when it comes to relationships. Awareness opens up an understanding of our strengths and weaknesses, allowing us to maximize the benefits of our gifts while seeking help in areas we need to improve.

Without awareness of our domestications and festering wounds, many people continue to make the same choices in their relationships, deal with the same types of issues, and ultimately find themselves in the same unhappy situations. Common phrases we've all heard or perhaps said ourselves point to this truth: "I keep dating the same kind of person." "Change the name and the face, but all my exes are the same." In order to break these patterns, we have to first become aware of them and their underlying causes.

Finally, if we don't nurture an ongoing awareness of our fears surrounding relationships, we may hold ourselves back from something we really want, stay in an unhealthy situation, or not speak our truth when the moment calls for it. We may sell ourselves short or settle for things that are less than what we really want, all because we are afraid to try or fear that we can't do better.

As you can see, awareness has many levels. The practice of awareness is simple to begin to learn and put to use, yet it will take a lifetime to master. It starts with watching your own mind and noticing its uncanny ability to make up stories about what it perceives.

Stories of the Mind

The importance of studying the mind has ancient roots in many spiritual traditions, including the ancient Native American Toltec tradition that we belong to.

According to oral tradition, the Toltecs came together over a thousand years ago in what is now Teotihuacán, Mexico, and one of the primary things the Toltecs studied was the mind's role in perception. They astutely recognized that the mind was constantly taking in information from all the senses and making up stories about what it perceived. They termed this habit of the mind "dreaming," because they realized that rather than perceiving actual reality, the mind was always interpreting its perceptions, adding judgments, making assumptions, ascribing meaning to actions and situations, etc. This meant that when a person's mind was at work, they were often living in their story about reality, aka a dream, rather than experiencing reality as it is.

When we apply the Toltecs' teachings to our modern lives, it becomes easy to see how our perceptions often don't accurately reflect reality. For instance, how many times have you made an assumption about your partner's beliefs or behavior only to learn later than it wasn't true? How often have you judged your partner for something you thought they had done and later found out that your judgment was incorrect?

Assumptions, judgments, and other mental activities all come together in the stories our mind cobbles together about what we perceive. The judgments and assumptions we make are based on a variety of things: our personalities, our past experiences, our hopes and wounds, and, of course, our unexplored domestications. One of the most prolific areas for story creation is in our relationships, and until we learn to spot and question our stories rather than believe them without investigation, these stories will continue to cause pain and suffering in our relationship.

Let's look at an example. We have a friend, Mark, who was in a relationship for about six months, and things were going very well. One evening, Mark's beloved texted him at the last minute and said he had to work late and he doubted he would be able to keep their date for the evening. Mark found this odd, because up until this point, he and Carlton had been in the new and magical stage of the relationship where they spent every possible moment together.

Then Mark remembered he had overheard a conversation that Carlton had had with his best friend where someone named Tom was mentioned. He didn't think much of it at the time, but now he began to wonder if there was more going on than he realized.

Over the next hour, Mark's mind spun an entire narrative about how Carlton could actually be out with Tom instead of working late like he'd said. This story was only exacerbated when Mark called Carlton's office and got the company voicemail.

Finally, Carlton called Mark late in the evening and said he was on his way over to the apartment. When he arrived, Mark's mood was reserved and skeptical, which cast a dark cloud over their time together. When Carlton finally questioned Mark about what was bothering him, Mark explained his concern that he wasn't at work but really out with Tom.

Fortunately for Mark, Carlton took this questioning very good-naturedly. He explained to Mark that he *was* at work, and Tom was someone his best friend was interested in dating. (Mark had even met Tom at a previous social engagement, but he hadn't put two and two together.) As you can imagine, if Mark had continued to believe the stories that his mind was telling him, they might have fought or even chosen to end their relationship, all because of a misperception of reality.

When we asked Mark why he thought he told himself a story that his partner was with someone else instead of at work, he explained that in a prior relationship his beloved had broken their agreement of monogamy by being with someone else. This had surprised and hurt him severely at the time and had caused a wound that he carried into his new relationships—it was this old wounding that provoked him to be skeptical of Carlton when he had to work late. Until Mark became aware of this old wound and the power it had over him, it resurfaced whenever he entered into a new relationship.

As this simple example demonstrates, our minds can create all kinds of judgments, make assumptions, take things personally, and tell stories about reality that, much of the time, don't fit the facts. Our past experiences, like in the case of our friend Mark, can heavily influence our stories in the present. Awareness is the practice of being able to recognize the difference between what is happening in the world and what is happening in our minds.

Many of the people we work with find that once they become aware of their own stories, they realize that some of the "problems" in their relationships are not caused by the actions of their partner but in the stories they tell themselves about those actions. In other words, sometimes it's not what our partner is doing that drives our negative emotions, but rather what we are thinking and telling ourselves about what they are doing. This thinking and storytelling are what cause us to suffer—not the action itself. Awareness allows us to separate facts of the behavior from our storytelling.

Zeroing In on Fear

Laced into our unhelpful stories is almost always a sense of fear, and for this reason it's no surprise that fear causes some of the most trying difficulties in relationships: fear of repeating past patterns, fear of being hurt, fear of not being enough. We are vulnerable to innumerable fears when we enter into the act of loving another and open ourselves to being loved in return. Awareness is a potent tool for working with fear. In fact, fears derive most of their power and influence when they are unspoken, secret, or unexplored. The simple act of unearthing your fears and becoming curious about how they manifest in your relationship is a first step to defeating this internal enemy.

There are two types of fear: physical and psychological. Physical fear is immediate, directly related to your current circumstances, and expressed in a full-body response. This is the fear you experience when you come face-to-face with a grizzly bear in the woods. Your heart rate rises, your body floods with adrenaline—you experience that fight-or-flight response. This physical fear, and your body's instantaneous reaction to it, will help your chances of surviving this meeting with a bear. It will make you faster, stronger, and more bold. Fortunately for most people, the majority of our fear in and around relationships is *not* physical fear.

Psychological fears are far more common. They can be subterranean, working in secret under the surface of our awareness and playing out in our domestication and our attempts to domesticate others. They can be long term, holding on to us over the course of months or years. And while these fears are based in the mind, they can still elicit some version of a fight-or-flight response in our bodies. When it comes to relationships, psychological fear manifests in any number of ways. These fears are connected to the stories of your thinking mind, as in, "I'm afraid this person will leave me," or "I'm afraid this relationship will fail," or "I'm afraid I am not enough." Psychological fear is the result of negative story creation. It goes without saying that when we are in the grip of these fears, they create some of the biggest obstacles to building and maintaining a happy and healthy relationship.

When we bring awareness—the third powerful secret of relationships—to these fears of the mind, we take the first step in drawing them out of the shadows and into the light of day, where we can learn to heal them.

For this reason, we want you to take a moment to make a list of all the specific fears you have about relationships. It may be an ongoing process to identify these fears, but as soon as you start you can begin to watch for the ways in which they manifest in your life. The list below provides a few examples of common fears that occur in relationships to get you started.

- I am afraid my partner will leave me.

- I am afraid my partner won't understand me.

- I am afraid my partner will fall out of love with me.

- I am afraid I will fall out of love with my partner.

- I am afraid I will be stuck in an unhappy relationship.

- I am afraid my partner will be unfaithful.

- I am afraid my partner won't forgive me.

- I am afraid I won't find a good partner.

- I am afraid I won't be a good partner.

Now it's your turn. What are some of the fears you have experienced around relationships? Some of these fears may be big, some may be small, but all are capable of sneaking up on you in your interactions with your beloved and can cause havoc until you are aware of them.

Once you have made your own list, you can reference it as you go deeper into awareness. You can locate where you feel each of these fears in your body or notice when and how they manifest in your life. You can investigate your reactions to each fear— through the stories you tell yourself, through the actions you take or don't take, through the things you say or remain silent about. At this point, you don't even need to work to change or correct these fears—for now, simply expand your awareness. There are a variety of methods to deal with these psychological fears, including healing our past, questioning our thinking, and having faith in ourselves, which we will explore in depth later.

For now, let's look at two common reactions that we have to psychological fear in our relationships, each of which can create negativity and emotional poison and block happiness and health: anger and closing off.

Anger

Anger is one of the most blatant ways that psychological fears present themselves. When you get angry, practicing awareness invites you to look within and discover what is happening inside of you. Anger is a secondary emotion, as it always hides fear or a sense of loss underneath it. Becoming angry often provides the feeling of being powerful—or, more accurately, the illusion of being powerful over others and even over ourselves. This is why some of us "like" to get angry. Being loud and abrasive is a method some of us use to make our point and to shut down the voices of others in the process. But of course this is a hollow victory, because the truth is that we can never have lasting power over others, even if we subjugate them in the short term, because ultimately we are all free.

The illusion of power as you enter a state of anger will often be followed by an emotional hangover, as you experience a variety of emotions such as shame, regret, blame, bitterness, and resentment, all as a result of your outburst. Anger often tempts us into saying or doing things that are hurtful or that we don't really mean, and neither of these reactions is helpful or conducive to a happy and healthy relationship.

When you find yourself beginning to get angry at your partner, stop and allow yourself to become aware of the anger. Locate where you feel it in your body. Is your throat constricting? Is your face flushing red and hot? Identify the thoughts associated with the anger, and any gradations of feeling. Label the feelings more specifically. Self-righteousness? Annoyance? Most importantly, uncover the psychological fear underneath these feelings. Train yourself to ask, "What am I afraid of in this situation? What do I want that I am afraid I won't get?" Or "what do I have that I am afraid I will lose? What story am I telling myself right now?"

It is *very difficult* to slow down in a moment of anger—in fact, it may feel totally counterintuitive—but we encourage you to give it a try. Asking these questions in moments of anger can provide a catalyst for insights that are less accessible in moments of calm. Getting curious about what is going on with you in the extremity of anger can tell you a lot about your underlying fears and the triggers for those big emotions.

Closing Off

The second most common reaction we have when we are fearful is to withdraw, shut down, or close off. While anger is a manifestation of our "fight" response, its counterpart of "flight" can manifest in any number of ways.

Many times, people close off in an effort to punish their partners by withdrawing their attention and affection. We also do it when we want to avoid or manage our fear or when we simply don't want to "rock the boat." However, as with an angry reaction, closing off is rarely helpful in terms of your relationships with others. Besides literally shutting down the curiosity and awareness that you need to move forward through any fear, it can also alienate your partner, making them feel as though you are disconnecting, ignoring, or even attacking them.

When we close ourselves off, our story-making mind often goes into overdrive, and as you can imagine, the stories it spins in these moments are even greater negative distortions of reality. We sulk and brood to ourselves, thinking of all the reasons why our partners shouldn't have said or done something. We blame, we punish, we imagine catastrophic outcomes. We may even have fantasy conversations with our partner and play out entire fights in our minds.

Here, again, awareness is key. If you find yourself shutting down, take a pause and ask yourself, "What am I afraid of?" Remind yourself that your mind is spinning a story. Rather than becoming an automatic believer of the story, engage your inner investigative journalist to ask the hard questions: "How am I really feeling right now? Why am I choosing to close off rather than deal directly with the situation at hand?" Again, there's no need to fix or change behavior right in this moment. At this point, simply being aware leads to a better understanding of yourself.

Does this mean that we should never step back and take a break? Not at all. Breaking the habit of closing off shouldn't be confused with a conscious decision to "take a break," which can be quite healthy and productive in relationships. In moments of extreme emotion, it can be helpful to distance yourself or take a break from a situation before you do or say something you might regret. The difference is in your intention and the energy behind your action. Listen for clarity of thought and a plan. If you are conscious and capable of saying, "I am taking a break from this situation and will return to finish it once I've cooled down," that is an entirely valid way of confronting a situation. This is very different from saying, for example "I don't know," "I don't care," or "Whatever you want." Taking a break with a plan to return with fresh eyes and a little perspective provides an alternative to hiding away or shutting down your own feelings and those of your partner.

Lastly, some people have what could be called a "freeze" response. Those of you who have experienced this know the feeling, as your limbs go numb, your mind goes blank, and you may also feel like your body can't move. This is often the case if you have suffered severe past trauma. If this describes you, it is vital that you be gentle with yourself as you begin to process and heal from these past events. You may also want to talk to your partner about the best way they can respond to you when you freeze, so that you can feel safe and come back into the moment and talk about what happened.

Emotions

In addition to noticing and identifying our fears, awareness serves to help us get more in touch with our emotions, as they can often provide a window into the inner truths that we may be hiding from the thinking mind. This is particularly true when it comes to uncovering emotional wounds.

For instance, we have a friend who would be overcome with emotion every time a divorce scene with children came up in a movie, even if it was a silly subplot. It didn't take him long to make the connection to his own lingering emotional charge related to the memory of his own divorce, as well as his parents' divorce. As he became more aware of those moments of being emotionally triggered, he was able to explore the underlying memories, which started the process of investigating and ultimately being able to release the power those emotions had over him.

When you are "randomly" overcome with big emotions, especially when your feelings seem out of proportion to the moment you're in, start to be cognizant of what is going on internally. This will help you find where you are still holding on to charges from past memories and serve as a reminder that you have more work to do to heal from them. Healing from a memory means that you can experience it without an overwhelming emotional charge. When you can hear about a similar situation or talk about yours freely without devolving into tears or getting so angry that it ruins the rest of your day, you are becoming free from it.

Those emotional triggers that you don't investigate and work through will fester and eventually find their way into your current relationship, as you project these unresolved emotions onto your unsuspecting partner.

Shadow Self

Because of our domestications, many of us have ideas about who we think we should be—and reject who we really are in the process. If our inner truth is not in alignment with the domesticated ideas of our minds, then an internal schism is created, and when faced with certain situations or choices, we may act or feel differently than we think we should.

If we continue to deny our own inner truth about something, then within our minds we are creating what we refer to as a *shadow self*. In other words, if we hold on to an image of who we think we are or who we think we should be, then any actions or desires that are contrary to this idea are relegated to our shadow, either by blinding ourselves to them or denying them.

In these cases, our actions and emotions can be the clues we need to show us what is really important to us. Intense emotions or actions that seem out of sync are flags and signals, and as we become aware of them, we can very often follow them to the source of the shadow self.

For instance, we know a couple, Joan and Sam, who had a firm agreement that after their first child was born, Joan would quit her job and stay home with their child. A few months after the baby's birth, it was clear to Sam that Joan was not happy being at home full-time with their newborn daughter. The arrangement was causing stress in their relationship because she was missing an outlet outside of the home. But here's the thing: Joan herself had trouble seeing this as a problem. While she admitted to missing her job and the break it provided from their child, she held firmly to the belief that "I am only a good mother if I stay home with my child," and she also believed that if she "just tried harder," then everything would eventually be fine and she would be happy as a stay-at-home mom.

Joan's idea of who she thought she *should* be was different from who she really *was*. When Joan and Sam discussed it and spent some time unpacking Joan's feelings, she realized that she had been domesticated to this idea as a child, but that it wasn't in fact true for her. She went back to work and was much happier. By becoming aware of this domesticated idea and the fact that it wasn't working for her, Joan was able to separate from her shadow and was freed to make a choice based on her own preference. Her relationship with Sam was healthier and happier as a result.

In another example, we have a student who came to us after a series of what seemed to be deep and promising relationships that would suddenly fall apart or turn unhealthy after a few months. She couldn't understand why she continually found herself in this "boom and bust" relationship cycle. As we discussed these relationships with her, she assured us that she always took her time before getting too serious. However, as we probed deeper into her last two relationships, she revealed some very telling behaviors. During her most recent relationship, she had moved in with her partner after just two weeks of dating, and in the relationship prior to that she had quit a promising job and taken a new one to align her schedule to her beloved's after only knowing each other for a few weeks.

To us, it was clear that there was a disconnect between how she saw herself, as someone who "takes things slow," and her actions and propensity for moving very quickly. This was her shadow in full force. It was easy for us to spot but difficult for her to realize until we pointed it out.

Finally, we had another student who had the notion on and off for years that he wanted a relationship that was polyamorous; that is, a relationship that extends beyond two people and can include a third or more people rather than a monogamous or "two-person only" relationship. When his monogamous relationship ended, he made a new agreement with himself that he would only date others who shared his preference for polyamorous relationships. But after a few months of dating this way, he began to notice that he wasn't very happy in this new style of relationship and in fact he missed more traditional monogamous roles. He had a fantasy ideal of himself that suggested that he act in one way, but the reality was that he was much happier in a traditional role. When he admitted this to himself, the inner schism went away.

As you work to reveal your shadow characteristics, you will gain a deeper understanding of yourself. The goal is to look at the differences between your ideas and beliefs and your behaviors, as the latter can often show you how you really feel about a situation. As a starting point, examine the places where you feel turbulent or uncomfortable emotions—those are often a big indicator of where you'll want to dig deeper.

Awareness of Your Partner's Reactions

As you gain awareness of yourself, you will often begin to see your partner's behaviors in a new light as well. You may begin to notice when your partner appears to be tilting off balance and reacting with words or actions that are not in line with what you know to be their best self. In these moments, rather than getting defensive or combative, awareness invites us to look deeper at our partner's behaviors and see if we can find out what their possible motives could be. For instance, are they reacting out of fear? If so, what might they be afraid of?

This takes a measured approach, because we can never know for sure what is going on in the mind of anyone else. However, our desire is to support our partner as much as possible, and this means looking at your partner's actions and behaviors with an understanding heart.

One couple we know, Anna and Pietro, recently shared with us something that often happens when they are packing for a trip. When there is a long list of things to do before they go, Anna in particular will become harried—racing around, dropping things, and snapping at the other members of the family as the clock ticks down to departure. This sometimes even extends into the car, when Anna becomes reactive to the behaviors of other drivers on the road. For years, this anxiety about leaving was a constant in their lives, and as you can imagine, it didn't make the rest of the family feel very excited about the start of a trip or vacation. It often led to arguments and resentments. Finally, Pietro gently probed Anna about what she thought might be going on. They talked about what underlying fears might be behind this behavior that was so out of character for his wife. She shared that she felt it was her job to make sure everyone had what they needed, and if they didn't have a good time on the trip, it would somehow be her fault. She felt as though she had to be as prepared as possible for all eventualities to save time and money and make sure everyone else was happy. But, he pointed out, this behavior was making them all miserable—her included. They agreed that they could make almost anything work and have fun if they knew they had a few essentials: each other, their wallets, and their phones. Everything else, Pietro would remind Anna, was gravy. This freed them both up to see their trips as adventures rather than minefields of potential failure and disappointment.

As we come to the end of the secret of awareness, we would like to add that while much of this lesson has been devoted to discussing how awareness can help you deal with "problems," awareness can also help you recognize what makes your heart sing, what brings you joy, what makes you happy. This is one of the great gifts of relationships, and one that we often forget—falling deeper in love through a moment-by-moment awareness within our partnership. We invite you to spend a few moments and reflect on these two questions:

1. What does your partner do that brings positive emotions and energy to you?

2. What do you do for your partner that makes you joyful?

Awareness can reignite the surprise and delight in your daily lives together. Once you know what makes you happy, it becomes easier to cultivate it. Awareness opens up a clear channel of desire that enables you to ask for what you want and need and respond to your partner's requests from a place of freedom and truth.

This is the great challenge and art of communicating, but for now, let's remember that for communication to be effective, we must be clear on our own wants, needs, fears, goals, hopes, and more. In order to nurture this clarity in our communication, we'll need awareness more than ever.

If it sounds impossibly optimistic that we can be fully clear about our motivations and desires before we communicate with our partners, do not fear. We can still communicate from a place of awareness even when our awareness is telling us that things aren't very clear at the moment. Awareness can allow us to say, "I don't know," or even "I don't know yet." There is great peace and beauty in the "don't know" mind. Embracing and admitting that we don't know is a much better place to be than believing the stories our mind is creating.

Explorations
Knowing Your Part
Cultivating deeper awareness in your relationships can help you to understand your part in any difficult situation or conflict. If you know where your stories and fears trigger your darkest shadow self, then it becomes your responsibility to ask for help.

Conversely, you can be aware of those times that you might be able to offer help to your partner in areas where they are struggling. In both cases, it's important to be clear about your responsibilities and to let go of what is not your responsibility. In this way, each partner can define and know their part. Here is a simple checklist of things to help you remember what your part is in a relationship:

Your responsibility:

+ What you say

+ What you do

+ What you think (or, more accurately, what you believe about your thinking)

Your partner's responsibility:

+ What they say

+ What they do

+ What they think

While this may seem simple, it can be very difficult to recall this list when you are enmeshed in emotions. Going through this list can bring you both back to basics.

Although relationships can really flourish when both partners practice awareness, we've noticed that even when only one person commits to this work, it can bring about amazing changes. When we claim our own part and change our behavior accordingly, it often tempers the reactions of others. It can even inspire a change in their behavior as well. After all, since it takes two to tango, it only takes one person to end the dance of conflict.

Think of a past conflict or exchange with your partner and make a list of your responsibilities. Consciously set aside any justifications for your actions based on their behavior. For example, instead of saying, "I yelled at him because he wasn't telling the whole truth," break it down into your actions and thoughts: "I yelled at him." "I felt betrayed and mistrustful." Think of the things you said and the actions you took. Looking back, was there something you could have done differently? Awareness is the first step to change.

What Bugs You?

"They really know how to push my buttons."

This phrase holds most true for our significant others, as no one knows how to push our buttons better than those close to us. Through the practice of awareness, we can watch our internal reactions to exterior stimulus, and in doing so we will learn more about ourselves. In other words, it's up to us to watch what buttons are getting pushed and how.

In what ways does your partner get on your nerves? When do you feel rejected by them? In what ways do they make you angry? In what situations do you react emotionally rather than respond consciously? Make a list of these moments. Remember that any reaction you are experiencing is inside of you, and you can work to experience the actions of the other as a gift that will help you find out what is going on inside of you.

Think back to the last time you experienced a big reaction to something your partner said or did. Where did that reaction come from? Is it based on your domesticated ideals? Past wounds?

Rather than immediately turning your attention to your partner's behavior in these instances from a stance of blame or self-righteousness, focus on awareness of the sensations in your own mind and body. Remember, their behavior may or may not be appropriate, but that is secondary when it comes to understanding your own reaction. The first step is to identify the reason for the emotional poison that is festering inside you. Doing so allows you to regain a state of calmness and clarity. From this place, you can accurately claim your part in any situation and approach your partner without judgment about any behavior they are doing that is hurtful. Awareness is how you know these are two different issues: your partner's behavior and your reaction to it.

THE
TRANSFORMATIVE
SECRETS

Chapter 4

The Secret of Healing

Asking the proper questions is the central action of transformation. Questions are the key that causes the secret doors of the psyche to swing open.
—Clarissa Pinkola Estés

Like it or not, no human being moves through this life immune to emotional pain. As we open ourselves to the full range of expression of our humanity, without a doubt we will all experience profound loss, betrayal, and other deep wounds. If we ignore these wounds and push them deeper inside us, perhaps pretending that they never occurred, the emotional pain will continue to fester and eventually erupt from our unconscious in the form of an emotional reaction. Even if we are proficient at hiding or suppressing these old wounds, this trapped negativity will keep us from experiencing all the joy that life has to offer. Healing reopens the energetic channel that connects us to our true selves, and by extension to others. In this way, bringing healing to ourselves is one of the most transformative things we can do to deepen our relationships.

In the last lesson we focused on the importance of awareness, because until we know ourselves and deal with what we find, it is very difficult to form a true partnership with another human being. In this chapter, we're going to take action on the gifts of our awareness and bring healing to any areas that need it, as until we start to heal ourselves from our past emotional wounds and unhelpful domestications, they will continue to sneak up on us and create fear in our minds. From this place of fear we react rather than respond, and we cause suffering in our minds and in our relationships in the process.

For some couples, the need to heal the past might not become apparent until we go beyond the first blush of love and settle into a place of security or steadiness. This is when we drop the images we are consciously or unconsciously portraying that have kept our wounds hidden. Or the need for healing might not present itself for many years, especially if the wounds are buried deep in the unconscious.

Whenever it arises, if you find yourself in a reactive, heavy, or fearful place in your relationship, you'll want to ask yourself two questions: (1) Is there a past emotional wound that is coming up in my current relationship? (2) Is there some idea, belief, or role I am maintaining that is no longer true for me? Oftentimes, both of these questions will apply to your situation.

One of our students shared a story of how she recognized that some of the struggles in her relationship were being fueled by experiences in her childhood:

> My father was in the military, so I was raised with really high, what I would call perfectionist, standards. When things didn't go well, or mistakes were made, he would often get angry, bark orders, and mete out punishment.
>
> As an adult I followed this pattern, and if I made a mistake or didn't meet a goal perfectly, I would often be exceptionally hard on myself. I also noticed that in certain areas, particularly those that reminded me of my father, I set some incredibly high

demands on my partner and would criticize him for not meeting my expectations.
Rather than being kind and understanding to my partner and myself when goals
weren't met or mistakes were made, I would
react with anger and judgment instead.

In this instance, our student's past experience
with a demanding parent left her domesticated to
the idea that perfectionism and an angry drill ser-
geant mentality were the best way to get things
done. Perhaps they were even linked in her mind
as an integral part of the expression of love within
a close family unit. But as she inflicted these ideas
on herself and her partner, they both suffered. Only
through her willingness to look at what was causing
these reactions was she able to identify—and ultimately heal—the wounds from her childhood.

Years ago, another friend of ours had recurring
difficulties with his wife around finances. It was a
constant source of conflict between them, in part
because his wife was very focused on accumulation
of wealth, while he admitted he was never very good
with money and would regularly make mistakes
in this area. Their marriage ended for a variety of

reasons, including differences in financial values. Many years later, as he was preparing to marry again, he noticed how he avoided any discussion with his fiancée about joint finances. Then, when she asked him a simple question about how they would handle the bills after the marriage, he exploded with a defensive reaction. He could tell by the look of hurt and surprise on her face that she hadn't meant anything critical when asking; for her it was just a simple question. He then realized that his reaction was based on the unresolved feelings around these memories from his first marriage and the story his mind was spinning as a result.

As these two simple examples illustrate, until we confront and heal from past experiences, as well as investigate any unhelpful ideas, beliefs, and roles we are playing that are the result of our domestications, we will continue to react from them, causing suffering to our partners and ourselves.

Healing the Past

All of us carry wounds from our past, from ordinary hurts to deep tragedies. Some of these will be easier to unearth than others, but they may include the suffering of a difficult childhood, a messy breakup or divorce, infidelity and untruths in relationships, emotional, mental, and even physical or sexual trauma (for yourself or those you love), or the death of a beloved.

Two emotions in particular can provide us with clues about where we need healing: shame and blame. These toxic feelings can poison your current relationship by dredging up events of the past. Really, they are two facets of the same impulse: shame is when we turn on ourselves directly and blame is when we use the actions or inactions of others to turn on ourselves indirectly. In either case, we are the ones who suffer.

You can begin the healing process by looking at any events or people that generate either a feeling of shame or a feeling of blame inside you right now. Once you have located the feeling, take some time to identify where you might be using your past experiences to hurt your present self. Ask yourself:

- What actions or choices in my past or current relationship do I continue to judge myself for?

- Where am I using other people's behavior in past relationships to keep myself down?

Your answers can help you to determine the wounds that need healing as you move forward in your present circumstances.

People who have spent a great deal of time exploring inner knowledge and working on their personal inward journeys have likely already dealt with, or at least identified, many of the big issues of their pasts. However, just like physical wounds, the landscape of the emotional body will always carry a scar. We have found that intimate relationships have the uncanny ability to reopen wounds that we think are well healed and to manifest them in new and unexpected ways as we go deeper into partnership with another person.

For instance, some of us have deep childhood wounds related to a lack of attention or affection from the adults in our lives at the time. When we are not seen for who we truly are as children, or if we were abused or witnessed abuse, the feelings we experienced then can continue to pop up later in our lives. Unconsciously we might try to fill what we perceive as holes (not enough affection, not enough attention) by seeking out whatever we didn't get as children in our intimate relationships as adults. Of course, no one else can fulfill or fix us in this way. A relationship may serve as a temporary bandage over the problem, but when we become aware of what needs to be repaired, we can begin the work of actually healing the wound ourselves.

Parallel and Opposite Behaviors

Until we heal ourselves from the wounds of our childhoods, we often unconsciously fall into what we call *parallel behavior* or *opposite behavior* patterns in our relationships as adults. A parallel behavior is when we mirror what was modeled for us as children, and an opposite behavior is when we embrace the opposite of what we were shown growing up.

Parallel Behaviors

A good example of parallel behavior is the student we mentioned earlier who adopted the military-style standards of her father and inflicted them on herself and her partner. In another example, one friend of ours described his first significant relationship this way: "I grew up in a house where drinking every night and shouting matches were the norm, so when my significant other drank heavily, I thought nothing of it. Once we got past the 'romance' period of the relationship, we fought regularly, and based on what I knew from my childhood, this was what serious relationships were all about." A person who witnessed controlling behavior by one parent over another might either pick a partner who controls them, or choose a partner they are able to control, continuing yet another damaging cycle. It's heart-breaking to see how even terribly destructive behaviors can elicit the warmth of familiarity for us.

Because these behaviors are so often learned from a young age, when they cannot be viewed as problematic or even as a choice, but simply as "the way things are," it becomes very easy to continue to play them out unconsciously later in life. Of the two types of unconscious behaviors, parallel behavior is often easier to identify because it is fairly straightforward in nature.

Opposite Behaviors

Opposite behavior, on the other hand, can be deceiving—presenting itself as a healing solution when in fact it may be deepening the wound further. For instance, we have a friend who witnessed his parents' verbal and sometimes physical abuse of one another, and as a result he swore he would never do that in his own relationship. Most of us can agree that this is a good vow to make. But the problem is that in an effort to keep the peace, he would remain quiet and push his true feelings down at any cost. He thought that avoiding confrontation was the only way to avoid abuse. Of course, this is also an unhealthy option, but in reaction to his childhood experiences he was going to the opposite extreme, silencing his voice in a way that cost him his own happiness through an unhealthy reaction to his parents' behavior.

In another common instance of opposite behavior, sometimes we intentionally seek out partners who we think are "nothing like" the parent we had difficulty with in our formative years, picking them based on who they are *not* rather than who they *are*. This is even a common trope in movies, when a child brings home a troubling future in-law to great parental consternation. Ironically, some people who have done this later realize that the person they thought was nothing like the parent they were trying to avoid was in fact very much like that parent. For example, as they get older, many a teenage rebel will be inclined to create the very kind of authoritative power they railed against in their youth. Obsession with power over others is a common thread between these two seemingly opposite personalities—rebel and authority.

The Hurt of Past Relationships

In addition to your childhood experiences, any emotional wounds that are still festering from your past intimate relationships can also find their way into your present one. For some of us, it feels like we are carrying the ghosts of our past partners along with us.

For instance, we may "defend" ourselves in our current relationship based on criticism we received from past partners, as in the case of our friend with wounds around finances. Even though he was having a conversation with his current beloved, the words coming out of his mouth were in response to a person who was long since gone.

When relationships end in conflict, betrayal, or infidelity, it can have a lasting impact on us. We can't help but feel that the relationship ended because it was "broken" in some way. Almost any divorce, and certainly any relationship that ends with the unexpected death of a beloved, has the potential to spell lasting trauma. In all of these cases, our initial happiness and hope for everlasting love has ended in the heartache of loss.

Past relationships that end in loss can be very difficult to release from our emotional centers, and oftentimes we bring them forward with us into a new relationship. As we engage with a partner after experiencing the loss of a beloved, we very often have the inclination to protect ourselves from any situation that might cause us to feel the same type of pain. This is a very powerful story of the mind that doesn't serve us well: we think that if we can anticipate hurt and imagine all potential catastrophes, we will protect ourselves. In fact, this story leads us to shut down our deepest connections, which are our best hope for health and happiness. After all, no one can build a safe and sturdy home on top of eggshells.

After the hurt of a past relationship, we may attempt to control others by withholding our love and affection. Or perhaps we take another route and withhold our vulnerability, only showing our partners who we are up to a certain point. We say to ourselves, consciously or unconsciously, "I won't expose myself completely because I don't want to be hurt." Once again, fear has found its way back into our relationship. The truth is that this fear of being hurt is also keeping us from opening ourselves to the full benefits of our current relationship. Here, again, healing can help us go beyond fear and allow us to experience the benefit of a deeper, fuller love without the unrealistic demand that the relationship should never have the power to hurt us.

In a potent example of how a past relationship can alter behavior, another dear friend of ours had an experience in his first marriage that he swore had "changed him forever." In this marriage, the relationship took a pronounced turn for the worse shortly after the birth of the couple's first child. Although they had been married for a few years when their son was born, his wife realized shortly after that motherhood wasn't her calling, and she wanted to leave the relationship to pursue her own life. Despite his pleas and their attempts at couples' counseling, she simply did not want the life they had developed, and she left him as the primary caregiver of their child. Our friend was heartbroken as a result, and he swore he would never marry or have children again.

A few years later, after dating a woman for a few months, and despite using birth control, his new beloved became pregnant. Our friend was immediately overcome with fear. While he loved being a parent of the child that he had, he was sure he did not want to go down this road again, as all he could see was heartache. But this time it was his new beloved who said to him, "I want to do this with you, but I will do it alone if I must." In this way, she and their unexpected pregnancy forced him to make a decision: grow or go.

Much to his surprise (but not to ours or hers), his experience with his new beloved was completely different than his first marriage, and we are now happy to say they have been together many years and have two additional children, plus the son from his first marriage. Just as importantly, he did a lot of healing and forgiveness as a result of this unplanned pregnancy, because he knew he needed to if his new relationship would have a chance. Our friend now laughs at himself when he thinks of his old plan of never marrying or having more children and says, "thankfully, life knew better than me."

Healing from Domesticated Ideas and Outdated Roles

Closely related to our past experiences of our childhood and prior relationships are the domesticated ideas that have been implanted inside us. These can haunt us in the same way that wounds from our past do and can similarly control our actions and reactions if we don't become aware of them and heal ourselves.

These domestications include old ideas and ingrained beliefs, as well as any roles we are playing that are keeping us from having the best relationship possible with our beloveds and ourselves. Almost all of us have adopted beliefs about relationships from our family, friends, religion, and even societal influences such as movies, TV, and books. Many of them are imprisoned in deep gender stereotypes. When we make these ideas our own, we begin to use them as tools of judgment on our partners and ourselves. For instance, here are some common domestications around relationships:

- Men should chase women, while women should play coy.

- Women should be emotional, and men should not share their feelings.

- Men should be the financial provider, and women should be the primary caretaker of children and home.

- Masculine energy is powerful and in control, while feminine energy is soft and supportive.

- Freedom in relationships is dangerous.

- The most important aspects of relationships are meant to be in service of raising families.

- If we don't retain an air of mystery, things will get boring.

These are just a few examples, and our point here is not to agree or disagree with these ideas, but simply help you notice which ideas might be implanted in your mind about the roles you should be playing. If the role is working for you, that's great. But for many of us in the modern world the roles are changing, so we want you to examine if any role or idea you have accepted matches your personal truth. If it doesn't, you will experience suffering and frustration around this area until you heal yourself from the need to play that role. Our friends Anna and Pietro in the previous chapter are a good example of this. Anna adopted the belief that it was her job to get everyone ready and make sure everyone had fun on their family trips, but because this was a role that she did not need to fill and that wasn't working for her, it made the trips difficult for everyone involved.

We also have a friend who, in her midsixties, decided she was no longer willing to do all the cooking and cleaning for herself and her partner. In her own words, she said, "I'm done with all of that." So she had to sit down and have a heart-to-heart talk with her partner and explain that the role of housewife and the duties that came along with it were no longer working for her and she couldn't keep it as a part of her life. As a result, they began to eat out more, they hired a housekeeper to come in every two weeks, and her partner also stepped up and took over half of the household duties. She used this newfound free time to take a part-time job outside the home, and this provided her with a new creative outlet. As a result, she is much, much happier. And so is her partner.

As you can see, a role that may have worked for us at one point in our lives won't necessarily work five, ten, or twenty years down the line. We want to repeat: we are not judging any idea, belief, or role. Our only concern is that they work for you. Problems arise when you adopt or maintain ideas and roles that are not true for you or are no longer true for you, whichever the case may be. Again, awareness is key, as many people will continue in the same roles in a relationship without realizing that the role no longer works for them. Once you become aware of the roles that you have adopted, consciously or not, you have an opportunity to heal from them.

Healing in the Current Relationship

At almost every relationship workshop we teach, there is at least one couple present that is attempting to heal from a serious betrayal of trust or infidelity. As a result, we are often asked if this is something that can be overcome and, if so, how.

First of all, we want to be clear that there is no one-size-fits-all answer to this question, as the details and specifics of each relationship are as complex and unique as the humans involved in them. That being said, we want to be clear that we *have* seen relationships recover and fully thrive after such instances, especially if both partners have a strong desire to heal. We have also seen couples separate in ways that, while painful, deeply served the growth and humanity of one or both parties.

When trust has been broken, it can be challenging to find the courage to rebuild. But if you have the willingness and ability to forgive, it is possible to deepen your relationship after a crisis like this. Most often, when it comes to an infidelity, our basic sense of justice kicks into gear. If you have experienced this, you may have noticed that your initial reaction was to balance the scales through punishing the offending party. Unfortunately, punishment will *not* deepen the relationship or help it get back on track. Withdrawing yourself from the relationship or from your partner as a form of punishment is unhelpful because in a sense it is another way of running or hiding from the problem. Your initial thought of "they don't deserve my time" is not helpful to healing the current situation, if that is your desire. Yes, there will be a time when you will feel the need to pull back or withdraw for personal reflection on your next steps, but it is important to be honest about how you are using this personal time. Are you using this space in a constructive way, or is it an act of punishing your partner or yourself?

Punishment is intended to inflict pain, but rather than alleviating the original hurt, it simply creates more pain in both parties. Punishment doesn't offer real progress toward either healing the relationship or reflecting honestly and choosing to leave. The longer we linger in punishment mode, the longer we put off the chance for true learning and growth.

Of course, if both parties are not on the same team and the betrayal keeps happening, then most likely the relationship can and should come to an end. In this instance, it will take some inner work to locate your deal breaker. This is the clear delineation of your boundary, or, put simply, what is okay and what is not okay for you. When this line is crossed, it may take all the courage you have to act, but you will know that when you do, the action you take is for the best for all parties involved, including others affected by a breakup such as children, family, etc.

We even know some people who have chosen to stay in a relationship even if betrayal or infidelity continues to occur. Their deal breakers are not located in that place for them. In the rare cases in which these relationships continue, the offended individual becomes even more focused on taking responsibility for their own happiness and has let go of any animosity toward their partner. They are not waiting for their partner to change because they know, ultimately, that their partner is responsible for their own decisions and actions, just as they are responsible only for their own actions. We have seen instances where those people who undertake this road find peace in their decision, and sometimes after many years of not attempting to force anyone else to change, a shift occurs in the other person spontaneously. To find your own path through these dark woods, it is important to ask: What is my choice? How do I want to live my life? What am I willing to do or not do?

The Healing Process

As we heal ourselves by recovering from past wounds and domesticated ideas, we also take an incredible burden off our existing partners, because until we heal ourselves, we will consciously or unconsciously look to our partners to fix us and to give us what we need. When they fail to make us feel better, we may even blame them. Of course, they can't "fix" us, because we are the only ones who can give ourselves the healing we truly need.

When we take responsibility for our own healing, we release the constant, searching attitude of "please fix me," and replace it with this instead: "I am whole, and I welcome your attention, encouragement, affection, and praise if and when you are in a place to provide it." When you heal yourself, you realize that your happiness and peace are no longer contingent on the constant support or adoration of others.

As you work toward healing your relationship with yourself, you can begin to work on healing your perceptions of your relationships with others, past and present. Notice that when it comes to others, we said it's time to heal your *perceptions* of those relationships rather than the actual relationships.

Why perceptions? There are two reasons: First, sometimes the actual relationship itself can't be healed—for example, if the person in question has died, or it's not safe or prudent for you to be in contact with them, or if they are unwilling to mend the relationship. Second, the most important thing you can heal, even beyond the relationship itself, is your internal story, or your perceptions of the past, because it's your thinking about these past events that brings up emotional poison as you relive the events again and again in your mind. In this way, you are punishing yourself with a charge of negative emotion every time that you rehash this old relationship, which no longer needs to have any bearing on your present or your future.

Forgiveness

Forgiveness is the most transformative tool we have for healing our wounds with ourselves, our parents, or other adults who raised us and the wounds from our past and present partners. Forgiveness is a multifaceted process that can range from letting go of hurt to resolution to wishing well for the offending party. It can go further and include a deeply spiritual practice by which we fully embrace our hurt and release the person who hurt us, clearing the way for complete absolution.

Most importantly, forgiveness allows for the release of the ongoing burden of pain. It clears our hearts to love ourselves and one another fully. When we hold our pain and suffering inside us, we build a dam that blocks the waters of unconditional love; but when we allow those waters to flow, we can find joy and renewed beauty in the places that our wounds have been healed.

We forgive because we want to enjoy the present and look forward to the future. We forgive because we are empowered to set aside the baggage of the past that only weighs us down. We don't forgive under duress or out of guilt, but because we understand that thoughts and feelings of resentment, grudges, and anger are, as the saying goes, the poison we administer to ourselves with the intent to hurt someone else.

Looking with kindness and loving compassion, we may see that the one who hurt us was confused rather than evil, that they were pursuing what they thought they wanted. We may look back at our own past, to the times we are ashamed of, and see ourselves with friendly eyes, as one who was lost rather than guilty, doing the best we could at the time.

Forgiveness is not just for the big things. Our current relationship can be weighed down with one hundred, one thousand, or ten thousand little things that we are holding against our partner and ourselves, and over time the weight of these little things can be just as damaging as large-scale traumatic events. They can sap the creativity, connection, and kindness from our everyday exchanges with our partner. Opening to forgiveness grants an opportunity to drop the load, to clear the air, and to address the little things that are blocking your happiness together.

Forgiveness is a beautiful ideal, but we have often heard people say, "I just can't forgive this person. The hurt is too deep." We understand these feelings and acknowledge that in many cases forgiveness is a difficult process, one that can't be rushed. At the same time, if this overwhelming pain applies to you, try setting aside the notion of saintly, absolute forgiveness. Along with it, kick to the curb any shame you are experiencing about wherever you are on your own personal forgiveness journey. Rather than trying to forgive all at once, all right now, simply ask yourself, what are you getting by holding on to your anger or resentment? We humans don't tend to do things for no reason. Maybe your pain is part of your identity, and releasing it feels terrifying? What are you afraid will happen if you *do* grant forgiveness? Will you be hurt again? Will you lose your self-respect? Your good judgment? Answering these questions can help you look deeper into the blocks that are preventing you from heading down the path of forgiveness and letting go.

Finally, we can't say enough about the importance of rituals when it comes to forgiveness and reclaiming your emotional power. To this end, we have included some rituals in the explorations portion of this chapter that can help you heal from old wounds, as well as change outmoded beliefs and ideas about yourself and the world that are keeping you trapped in the past. Rituals are an outward expression of your inner intent to heal. In this way, healing becomes more than just something you think about. Through rituals, you bring the power of action to support your intent. Many of our students and friends have expressed major breakthroughs in their current relationships when they were able to extend forgiveness fully, and in all directions, through the use of rituals.

In one case, a friend of ours chose to perform a forgiveness ritual in a city park—the place where, years before, and much to her surprise, her beloved had ended their relationship. Not only was she upset over the breakup, but she also drove past this park regularly, and every time she did she remembered that day and felt a surge of emotions. She decided the best way for her to heal was with a forgiveness ritual (included as the second exercise at the end of this chapter), which she undertook at the very spot in the park where the news was delivered. She explained later that not only did she feel incredible relief as a result of the ritual, but she also reclaimed her emotional power around the park. Now when she drives by the park it is a profound reminder of her own power to forgive and transform through active healing.

Explorations

We've covered a lot of ground in our discussion of forgiveness, and yet these broad strokes form the most basic steps of the healing journey. There are a great many avenues to healing, and every person's journey will be different. With that in mind, let's focus on the healing techniques that have been most helpful to our students and us. If the following healing practices don't resonate with you, continue to search until you find ones that do. Remember: the most valuable gift you can give yourself and your partner is to take responsibility for your own healing.

Healing List

On a piece of paper, list the ideas from your childhood or past relationships that you once believed but now recognize (or suspect) are no longer true for you. The purpose here is not to blame or shame, but rather to make an assessment so that you can notice what needs to be healed now. Here are a few examples:

My Perception of Events	Result
My father was a heavy drinker and gone a lot. He missed many of my important events.	I sometimes crave attention, recognition, and I have a strong need for others to be there at events that are important to me.
The adults in my life argued loudly and were verbally abusive to one another.	I dislike loud conversations, even if they are not abusive. I avoid confrontation to an unhealthy degree.
My previous partner cheated on me.	I am paranoid that my current partner will do the same, to the point that I can be overbearing or controlling of their actions.
My mother was not affectionate.	I sometimes crave physical touch and can rush in or overlook other things if I get caught up in my desire for physical connection.

This exercise strengthens our awareness, and begins the healing process simply by labeling our unhealed wounds. Just as importantly, it can give us a jumping-off point to apply to the forgiveness exercises that follow.

Forgiveness Ritual

On a sheet of paper, list every person you feel has mistreated you and you have not yet forgiven.

Review the list of names one by one and think briefly about the incidents involved with each.

Next, read the following statement out loud:

> *I,_____, am making room to forgive all those who inflicted pain and suffering on me in the past. I choose to forgive them so that their actions of the past can no longer affect my present. My wish is to see them through the eyes of unconditional love. I also forgive myself for anything and everything related to these events. I was doing my best at the time. I pray that these people, and myself, can experience love and peace going forward.*

When the pain inflicted by others is extreme, an act of forgiveness is rarely a onetime event. As a result, the aforementioned statement can be a tool, repeated every time the events of your past replay in your mind and you feel the negative charge of emotion as your mind tries to lead you down the road of negativity and conditional love.

If there is someone on the list whom you are having particular trouble forgiving, say the prayer below every night before you go to bed, inserting their name:

I pray that _____ receives everything they want in life, including the experience of unconditional love, peace, and happiness.

You may have bristled at this, as the prospect of praying that the person who hurt you receives love and everything they want is perhaps the opposite of what you think you want for them. We understand feeling this way and would still encourage you to give this prayer a chance. Repeat it every night for two weeks, even if the words don't feel sincere. Many people who have done this exercise consistently for two weeks have been amazed by the changes that occur inside them around their previous hurts. This prayer opens up an alternative to the fantasies of punishment that can consume and imprison us.

Remember, forgiving others is something you're doing for yourself, not for them. Forgiveness does not mean that you forget the events of the past or that you condone any actions; rather, it frees you from being controlled by them.

Forgiveness Dialogue

This exercise consists of two written parts, each about a paragraph in length.

PART 1

To begin, look back at a past relationship and identify an event or situation when you experienced significant suffering at the hands of another. This could be a past intimate relationship or a relationship with a parent, but it should be a major event that changed the way you viewed the other person and the world.

Write down the details of the event as if you are telling someone who has no previous knowledge of it. Take your time and replay the specifics in your mind, going back to that moment so you can remember what happened. Meditate on how it moved through your body, what you were thinking, how you felt, and what you did. Here is the important part: write from your perspective *at the time*, not from where you are now. Be raw and in the moment, let your feelings flow, and do not edit yourself with knowledge of what is right and wrong, or try to be forgiving. Remember, this exercise is for you, and unless you choose to share this with someone else, you will be the only person who ever sees it.

Here is an example from one of our students:

I left the house one morning for work as I usually do and had driven about fifteen minutes when I realized I had left something I needed for a presentation that day back at home. I turned the car around to go back and pick it up. It was at most twenty-five minutes total before I was back home.

When I pulled into the drive, I saw that my fiancé's car was still in the garage, but there was another car parked out front that looked like one a female coworker of his drove. I thought this was odd and wondered what she would be doing here, especially

when it was just my fiancé at home. I immediately had a sinking feeling in my gut.

I quietly opened the front door and
hesitantly entered my home. It's hard to
describe the odd feeling of unease and near
panic I was feeling on one hand, while
another part of me, my thinking mind, kept
saying that there would be a logical explana-
tion for it all. No one was in the front of the
house, so I walked down the hall towards
the bedrooms, and I could hear the shower
running as I got closer.

The next part makes me want to vomit,
but I could hear my fiancé moaning loudly
as they were having sex in our shower, in
the home that we shared, just a few weeks
before we were to be married. I walked into
the bathroom and stared at them through
the glass door of the shower. My voice dis-
appeared and my emotions were turned
inside out. I stood there for a few seconds
in silence until she saw me and screamed.
My fiancé then looked at me and immediately blurted out something about what

was I doing back at home. I turned around and just left the house, sobbing.

I remember feeling so disgusted with him and her, and yet also disappointed in myself. How could I have not seen this? Was I somehow not good enough for him? Thoughts and feelings rushed over me as I ran out of the house and drove away, my fiancé calling my name as I left. Over the next few weeks I found out that my fiancé had been with other women as well. I broke off the engagement and moved back into my parents' house.

In this example, our student was not only crushed by the actions of her fiancé, but she also used this as a reason to turn on herself and berated herself for "not being enough." Your past event might not be as dramatic as this, or it could be more dramatic. To get the most out of this exercise, we encourage you to not read any further until you have written down the example in your own life. Once you have, come back and continue with the exercise.

PART 2

This next part involves your imagination, as you want to heal your perception of your relationship with others.

First, imagine that you are meeting the person who hurt you—but in their spiritual form only. In this form, you can say whatever you want without fear. Tell them how you really feel about them and the situation.

Here is our student's example:

> Jim, I am so angry and saddened by what happened. I can't believe you would cheat on me. We were together for five years. I thought you were my best friend. I also blamed myself afterwards, thinking that somehow I was the cause of your cheating. I struggled with this for a long time, asking myself what I could have done differently to prevent this.

Next, try to imagine what this person would say to you, and—this might be tricky—only what they would say to you from a place of unconditional love. This will be difficult, but it invites you to tap into the power of compassion and kindness, and to try on the notion of that love coming from them to you. Write the dialogue that happens in your imagination between the two of you.

Here is our student's example:

> I am so sorry for hurting you, Beth. What I did was completely inappropriate. I am so sorry you saw us, and I know that image is difficult to get out of your mind. You were a wonderful friend and companion, and the truth is I don't fully understand why I did what I did, but I do know that it had nothing to do with you. Please forgive me and let me go. I want you to move on with your life and be happy. When you remember me, I hope you can find a way to remember the good times we had together and not this awful event at the end. I love you always and ask for your forgiveness.

This exercise allows you to get in touch with your feelings at the time, express them, and then listen to a loving response from the other person.

Forgiveness Ceremony for Couples

If your partner is open to it, you may want to try what we call a forgiveness ceremony, which has its roots in an ancient African tradition where spouses come together to forgive each other of their trespasses and start anew.

One at a time, each person shares their upset and frustrations with their partner. They scream, they moan, they whine. One person speaks at a time, letting everything out, while the other partner listens without saying anything. Then they switch. After each person has exhausted their complaints, they sit quietly and embrace each other. The embrace means that they both agree to wash away the grievances they shared.

Chapter 5

The Secret of Joy

Love doesn't just sit there, like a stone, it has to be made,
like bread; remade all the time, made new.
—Ursula K. Le Guin

At our lectures and workshops, couples often approach us with a familiar story. They have been together for some time, they don't doubt their love for one another, there hasn't been any major traumatic event or trust-breaking issue such as infidelity, yet they nevertheless feel like the spark has either dimmed or even gone out in their relationship.

Some of these pairs are the parents of young children that take up much of their time; for others it could be busy work schedules or the obligations of taking care of an aging parent. All these couples share the common issue of not feeling as connected or energized toward each other as they once did, and they are worried that their relationship might never be as good as it once was.

To make matters worse, this lack of energetic connection often extends into a couple's time in the bedroom. Where there was once strong chemistry, things now seem routine and dull. While the specifics of each relationship vary, couples in this situation basically ask the same questions: How do we rekindle the fire we once had? What can we do to bring that feeling of joy back to our relationship?

Questions like these bring us to the next transformative secret of happy and healthy relationships: joy. For most of us, the pursuit of joy is what led us to choose being in a relationship in the first place. Certainly we'd all like to experience joy when we think of our relationship.

Going deeper, can we understand more about the nature of joy? What does it mean in the context of relationships to crave joy or find it lacking? How does joy function in our lives? Joy contains multitudes: curiosity, connection, surprise, ease, pride, bliss, humor, and hope. It manifests in us when we are openhearted, present, and fully engaged. Think of a child in a moment of wonder—maybe when she sees an ocean for the first time—or when a baby finds something funny and lets loose with an infectious belly laugh. Without joy, we are shadows of our true selves: closed, cold, fearful, and ungrateful.

Joy is placed after healing because if we refuse to allow ourselves to look at, feel, and heal from our emotional pain, we cannot fully release into joy. Though it might seem counterintuitive, joy thrives in the full experience of life. We can't shut down or hide our pain without also shutting down joy. So while most of this chapter is focused on ways we can bring more joy into our lives, we also want to point out that it's through honoring all our experiences and emotions (even the ones that don't feel so good) that we open the floodgates to more delicious joy.

Practically speaking, there are three concrete ways to cultivate joy in your relationship: creativity, curiosity and play, and sexual pleasure.

Creativity

The first way to cultivate a feeling of joy in your relationship is through creativity. When we say this at our workshops, there is always someone who speaks up right away and says, "but I am not a creative person!" To us, nothing could be farther from the truth. Saying "I am not creative" is the equivalent of saying

"I am not a human." In our minds, neither of these statements makes any sense.

The truth is that human beings are the most prolific creators on the planet. We are all creating every day, even though many of us don't think of it that way. Take a moment to consider all the things humans have created where there once was nothing. From the buildings that house us to the technologies that connect us to the systems of commerce that support us to the laws that allow us to coexist, our creativity is everywhere.

Think of your own home and professional life. What have you created in these areas? A loving relationship or family? A job well done for your clients or employer? Have you ever made a special meal, written a heartfelt note, or planted a garden? Once we begin to value the creativity we utilize every day, we start to see that when it comes to human imagination, the possibilities are endless. Even our language itself tells us that we cannot help but create the world as a means to understand it. Think of our metaphors: "I'm feeling blue," or "let's have a blast tonight!" We create the world around us as we think and speak—in color, sound, and energetic vibrations. We only have to notice it to start to harness our creative powers.

We certainly understand what people mean when they utter the words "I am not creative." In this context they are often reserving the word *creative* for someone who deals in the traditional arts, or they tell us they aren't creative because they don't typically come up with new ideas or think outside the box. However, every human is an artist. This truth was abundantly evident to the ancient Toltecs, too, as the word *Toltec* actually means "artist." In their view (as well as ours), all humans are artists, and our art is expressed in how we create the story of our lives.

Something amazing happens when we *consciously* create things in our lives, as doing so can make you feel alive and connected in a way that nothing else will. Consciously creating means that you set out with the intention of doing or making something new, something that the very process of doing excites you and makes your heart sing. We can certainly feel this way by painting, sculpting, writing, or making music, but also through cooking, sewing, dancing, drawing, quilting, woodworking, or learning a new skill or hobby.

As children we were naturally creative and spent a large portion of our days coloring, making things, dancing, and singing. As we grew older, we discarded many of these things, especially if others told us things like "you aren't creative" and we believed them. Consciously creating is a way to reconnect with the fascination of life and the joy we felt in our most imaginative moments as children.

Turning back to relationships, so many of the couples we work with have forgotten about the magic of creativity. When a relationship begins, you are creating something new together, even if you don't realize it or label it as such. Just the very process of building a relationship together is creative: you are trying new things, growing in love and trust with one another, and perhaps even embarking on bigger creations like a marriage or children.

But for many couples later on in the relationship, things change and we forget about that creative spark. The routines of life take over, and the responsibilities of being a householder set in: jobs, children, chores, bills—all of which feel more "important." What once was new now feels monotonous, and some of us even question if the relationship was ever right in the first place.

Whenever you are feeling dried up and depleted, the trick is to bring the power of creativity back into your partnership. Tap into this special energy and channel it into new projects or hobbies. The possibilities are limitless. You can create in areas that you are both passionate about, or even better, you might check in with each other about some new things that you want to experiment with together and discover new passions along the way. It might take a little bit of gumption to jump-start some creativity with your partner, but the joyful reward will be worth it.

To start you off, think of it this way. Creativity in your relationship can be sparked in one of two ways: by doing something new or doing something old in a new way. So even if you're not ready to take on a whole new creative endeavor, you can slyly revamp your existing activities.

What can you and your partner do together that is new and potentially exciting for both of you? What is the sweet spot of your connection to each other? If you love to eat delicious food, try taking a cooking class! Learn to salsa! Find a weekend day trip. Try a fitness class that neither of you has attempted before. Take up bird-watching. Read a book out loud together. Our only suggestion is that whatever you choose, make it something that is truly new and enjoyable for both of you. (For example, if you have always wanted to take up auto racing but your partner hates moving fast, this is probably a good hobby for you to take up on your own.)

If you aren't quite ready to go skydiving together, you can get the same benefits from bringing a sense of newness to your existing activities. Change it up. Head to new restaurants instead of the usual places. Try a new TV series or movie together. Sleep on your partner's side of the bed for a few days. Even a simple switcheroo like that can bring a moment of joy. Some of our favorite family meals as kids were impromptu pancakes at dinnertime. It can be especially meaningful to your partner to take a little time to think of something special you did when you first met and bring it back in a new way. If you brought your partner red roses, you might send them purple ones now, with a note about how you feel as your love deepens and grows over time. A gesture like this serves as a reminder of your past love while keeping it new and creative.

When we reintroduce creativity into our relationships, as well as our own individual lives, we can find the hidden treasure of joy that we buried as children.

Curiosity and Play

So often, we get into trouble in our relationships when we think we already know what's going on with our partner or ourselves. This can lead to a kind of rigidity in our thinking and in our interactions with those we love the most. And the more time we spend together, the more we can be tricked into believing that we have a big enough body of knowledge to "really know what's going on." When we catch ourselves thinking this way, especially if our relationship is feeling a bit stale, it's time to recommit to curiosity.

One of the easiest ways to do this is to ask questions. While we often ask questions of our partners when the relationship is new, if we aren't careful, we can forget this important practice as a relationship matures. Questions are a way of signaling to your partner that you want to know about them, and this can immediately heighten your connection. Those that start with "how" or "what" are often open-ended and particularly effective: "How do you feel about XYZ?" "What would you like to do this evening?" "How did things go at work today?" and as a bonus question, "How can I help you see how beautiful you really are?"

You can also bring a sense of curiosity into your daily interactions, and design little experiments or challenges to do with your partner: "What happens if I plant a kiss on my beloved every time we're in the kitchen?" "How does it feel to ask for, and receive, a hand or foot massage?" "How many times can we take walks together in one week?"

Curiosity requires an open heart, a generosity of spirit, and true physical and mental presence. Curiosity opens the door to new avenues of creativity. It's important to note here that curiosity is also a powerful tool to deal with pain and to move through difficulty in transformation. When you or your partner, or the pair of you, is in the midst of suffering, try reaching out with compassion and ask, "What's really going on right now? What is up with me, or us? How are we feeling in our hearts and minds in this moment?" The answers to these questions may not be easy, but they will take you into new, fertile territory and increase your connection with one another.

The next ingredient in the recipe for joy is bringing a sense of play to your relationship. Like being creative, playing is one of the childhood pastimes that we most enjoyed but have a tendency to push to the side as we grow older. Play is replaced with work, school, responsibilities, exercise, and even things like spiritual practice or self-improvement. All of these adult activities are fine and good, but we also want to make sure we are reserving time for pure fun, too—especially when it comes to our partners.

When we get too serious about the activities of life, this can spill over and dampen the flame of our relationship. Playing together is a surefire way to stay clear of the relationship doldrums. Like it or not, boredom is one of the top reasons why relationships ultimately end, which occurs when we take each other for granted. It's not the final straw, but rather one of the first, as it sets the stage for loss of connection, disillusionment, and even betrayal.

Sometimes the solution is as simple as a good belly laugh between you and your partner, which can create joy in a way that nothing else can. When it comes to play, we suggest picking something that is just for fun. Seriously! It's important to find some activities that you're not doing to accomplish anything or improve yourself in any way—you're just doing it for the pure feeling of joy that it brings.

While we want you and your partner to play individually as part of the first two secrets (committing to yourself and extending freedom to your partner), we're talking now about some joint play-time. Focus on finding fun things that you can do together. Remember, your partner is one of your closest friends, if not your best friend, so including this person in your fun is an important part of cultivating joy in the relationship.

One couple we know went so far as to make a dining room table that doubled as a place to play table tennis. They asked a carpenter friend to make a solid wood table with some nifty hardware on the sides that allowed them to quickly install a net whenever they wanted. As soon as the dishes were cleared, instant fun!

If you have been in a relationship for a long time and find you're in a rut, seeking new ways that you can play together can spark the fire. While much of our discussion of relationships focuses on serious issues, we can't overstate the importance of making time for fun. Life happens. Plans change. Finding a way to laugh and have fun in the midst of it all can remind you and your partner of why you are together in the first place.

As an added benefit, once you cultivate more playful time with your partner, you may find that this sense of play also enters the bedroom, which leads us to our next element of joy: sexual pleasure.

Sexual Pleasure

For the vast majority of couples, sex is a vital component of creating joy in the relationship. For monogamous couples, sex is often a sacred activity you reserve for just you and your intimate partner. There are few things in a relationship that are more bonding and empowering than enthusiastic, connected, passionate sex. And there are few things more isolating than frustrating, one-sided sex—or a lack of sex at all.

Most relationships start in a hormonal soup of pleasure and connection. We can't get enough of our beloved, and everything they do brings joy. But as the relationship matures, almost every couple we know has experienced high and low points to the sexual aspect of their relationship.

Some low points can't be avoided due to the nature of life (illnesses, responsibilities to others, emergencies, and the like), but a healthy and happy relationship will typically bounce back from these quickly and naturally with a bit of extra care and attention. When this low point becomes prolonged, however, it's time to see if any other issues are getting in the way, including any of your domesticated beliefs. In our experience, after the initial hormonal period wears off (and sometimes much later), these beliefs are the main culprits that can creep back in and block you from receiving the joy that a good sexual relationship can give.

Like other areas of our lives that we have already covered, our domesticated ideas around sex can create all sorts of internal struggles, well before we even get to the bedroom. Furthermore, many people believe the issues they have with sexuality are unique to them, or "personal problems," but what we have learned as teachers as well as adults on our own personal journeys is that every human we have ever encountered has experienced issues with sex in one form or another, most of which stem from these domesticated ideas.

When it comes to sex, we call these domesticated ideas "common sex myths," so before we discuss any more about how to reclaim the joy in your sexual relationship, let's cover some of the more prevalent myths that cause issues in the couples we counsel:

- One must look a certain way to be sexy.

- One must maintain or have a certain body type to be sexy.

- Women don't enjoy sex as much as men.

- A woman's primary role is to please the man during sex.

- People should just know how to please their partner (without any guidance or instruction).

- Men want sex more than women.

- Having sex with a person of the same sex is wrong or dangerous.

- Once you go through menopause, you won't enjoy sex.

- Certain sex acts should never be performed even if all parties are educated and consenting.

- You should be sexual with your partner even if you don't want to.

- If you were sexually abused, you'll never be able to enjoy sex.

- If you have sex with more than one person, you are a "slut" or a "player."

- If you can't keep an erection, you should be ashamed, and there is no point having sex.

- The older you get, the less you enjoy sex.

Believing these myths, even unconsciously, can change the way you view your relationship with your partner and how you approach your sexual relationships. Domesticated beliefs in the area of sex run very deep, making it hard to see them as beliefs instead of "the way things are." For instance, in our workshops there is almost always someone who will claim that one or more of the things on this list are objectively true and not myths at all. They say something like, "Well, I read an article that said men do want sex more than women." Our response to this is always, "Do you believe that because it's true? Or is it true for you because you believe it?"

What we mean with this response is that when we maintain beliefs that are based on blanket statements that have been upheld for a long time, we have trouble seeing them as beliefs, and we mistake them for facts. So as we begin this exploration into sex, we invite you to become familiar with your own beliefs about sex and how they may be affecting your sex life.

Sex is far more mental than most people realize, and this is quite easy to prove and experience on your own. For instance, a thought about sex, not to mention a full daydream about sexual acts, can stimulate your body and increase blood flow to your sexual organs, producing an erection or vaginal secretions. No physical touching is necessary for this to happen; *it is all a result of what you are thinking*. So for many sex issues, changing your thinking about sex is just as important as changing any physical behavior. How you think about sex is just as important as what you do.

As we unpack some of these mental myths, we can come into a new relationship with sexual pleasure. No matter where you are in your relationship dance, from a budding romance to a long-term partnership, understanding the connection between your mind and your sexuality can help you keep your sensual garden in bloom.

To begin, we will focus on what we call the three *p*'s: permission, presence, and practice. These tools can help us undo any mental blocks and old domestications we have about sex, revitalize and energize our sex lives with our partners, and bring joy to our relationship in the process.

Permission

Your body is capable of experiencing sexual pleasure.

This bears repeating.

Your body is capable of experiencing sexual pleasure.

The question is, do you give yourself permission to have sexual pleasure? While many people are pretty sure they allow for sexual pleasure, a deeper search often reveals that there are unconscious voices in our heads, born out of domestication, that tell us sexual pleasure is wrong, selfish, or even dirty. As a result, some of us have deep-seated notions of shame or guilt around sex that are continually reinforced by a complicated mind-set about sex in our society.[1]

We are bombarded with mixed messages about sex, sexuality, and sensuality—from media, religion,

---

[1] It should be noted that having domesticated issues around sex that prevent you from feeling sexual pleasure is different than some people's experience of having no desire for sexual interactions. An individual who is asexual may have no desire to have sex and no sex drive that motivates them to have sex, whereas another person may have the desire for sex but difficulties in experiencing sexual pleasure. For the purposes of our discussions, we will be focusing on those who do wish to have sex but have blocks in regards to receiving sexual pleasure due to their domestications and ingrained mind-sets.

family beliefs, and even scientific research. We are rated "good" or "bad" as people according to sexual and gendered standards, from being a chaste "good girl" to being prized for being "good in bed," to getting lionized for being a sexy "bad boy" or respected as an upstanding, protective "good man." All of these are layered with values and judgments that we cannot escape without unpacking them. Further, the very idea of pleasure, which we understand to be fundamentally "good," can turn on a dime. If it's "sensual pleasure," the feeling becomes much more tricky—connoting hedonism and self-gratification. This underlying message that links pleasure with dangerous indulgence can block our efforts to explore the joys of sex in healthy ways.

We also withdraw permission for pleasure when we are ashamed of our bodies. For instance, if you regularly judge or reject your body for not being "enough" in some way, you are also subtly programming your mind to reject your body when it comes to sexual pleasure. While we strongly encourage you (and everyone!) to love and accept your body just as it is, we understand that this is very difficult for many people.

That being said, begin by simply noticing the connection between what you think about your body and how it can affect your sex life. If you are berating or not accepting your body as it is, then it gets very difficult to feel sexy or even fully comfortable naked in front of your partner. As a result, your thinking about your body can already dampen the mood before any sexual activity has even begun.

If this sounds like you, work on noticing this and say to yourself, "I love my body as it is, and I give myself permission to experience pleasure." This can get you headed in a different direction. Your thinking mind may still voice its opinion, but simply becoming aware of it is the first step to recognizing the mind's ranting as unhelpful opinions rather than facts. The truth is that your body is perfect as it is, right now, and you deserve pleasure regardless of your pants size, or how your thighs look, or the shape of your tummy, or the amount and location of your body hair. Keep turning your attention away from judging your body to honoring and inviting your capacity for pleasure.

Also, be sure to give yourself permission to explore pleasure on your own. Sometimes we get stuck in the false belief that we can only have pleasure when we have a partner. Explore your body and learn what, where, and how you like to be touched. Create space to give yourself permission for pleasure, as you will need this in a later *P*, practice!

Presence

Pleasure also requires your full presence. If you are distracted, trying to control the situation, or fixated on wanting to please the other person, you will not be present and available for your own pleasure.

Sexual presence is about engaging your attention in your senses, in this moment. If we engage in sexual activity worrying if we will do it right or worrying about our bodies not looking the way we want them to, then we are out of the moment and into our heads. Sometimes we might still be preoccupied with events from earlier in the day or thinking about what we have to do tomorrow, both of which take us out of the present. In this case, we can gently bring ourselves back to the present moment by noticing our breath and tuning in to our senses. We also suggest turning your phone or other electronic distractions off for at least thirty minutes prior to sexual activity, as doing so can help you ground into the moment. Technology is wonderful, but it is mind stuff, and in most cases it takes us away from our bodies and what is happening in the present moment.

All of these examples demonstrate the mind's ability to influence our attitudes and behaviors toward sex in the moments just before the act itself. Instead of following the blur of your thoughts, we invite you to center your awareness in your body as you prepare for sex. Bring your attention down from your head and really feel the various parts of your body: your feet and legs, your hands, arms, torso, and, of course, your genitalia. Next, we invite you to pay attention to your surroundings, as this too can ground you in presence. What colors are your eyes drinking in? What smells, tastes, and sensations are happening in this intersection of time and space that will never occur again?

Sometimes you may find that when you show up more with your partner, they have a hard time meeting you. Or sometimes you'll notice that your partner shows up more fully when you are distracted. Physical intimacy leads to emotional intimacy, and sometimes we fear being truly seen by another. The fastest path to intimacy comes through naked vulnerability, both physical and emotional. Connecting fully with your partner in the present moment is what will cultivate joy in your sex life.

One final note on presence: don't withdraw your presence after the climax portion of the sexual encounter is over. Science has shown that orgasms release the chemical dopamine in our brain and a little snuggling afterward releases the hormone oxytocin. Both of these are part of what makes you feel physically great during and just after sex, which is another reason to be present and enjoy the moment. Many couples say they feel a stronger bond with each other if they cuddle after sex, one that extends into the rest of the day. If you don't do this with your partner already, give it a try and see how it feels!

Practice

Your body is an instrument of pleasure, and once you have given yourself permission to experience that pleasure and are grounded in the moment, you will want to learn the ins and outs of your instrument in order to play the best music. Plus, you will need to practice, practice, practice. When we are young, our body is like a brand-new instrument, but we are inexperienced musicians. As we age, gain experience, and learn how to fine-tune it, the sound can become richer and more resonant. We invite you to see yourself as a musician and your body as your favorite instrument, ready to improvise, learn new riffs, and tend to your music.

Another way our mind limits our sexuality is by telling us that we "know" all about sex and how to give our partners or ourselves pleasure. As we discussed in the section on curiosity, the problem with this type of thinking is the minute we think we know something, we close our minds to learning or experimenting with anything new. When it comes to sex, we encourage you to never take the position of an expert, but rather maintain the mind-set of beginner instead. Approach it as something you can always learn more about, and be willing to try new positions, roles, and techniques. Ask questions of yourself and your partner, using "how" questions to open up discussion. Give feedback. Create an atmosphere of curious exploration. There are numerous books and videos just for this purpose, and we encourage you to look into some of these for ideas about ways you can grow. Reviewing this material might make you feel uncomfortable or even "dirty." If you experience any of that on this journey, remind yourself that this is a voice of domestication, and see if you can heal yourself from it.

The benefits of learning something new can be tremendous, as one of our friends explains:

> I was actually in a relationship for a while with a sex therapist, and he had a very intimate knowledge of women's anatomy and pleasure. In this relationship I discovered that my body had way more capacity than I realized. When I began dating the man who is now my husband, I wanted to share with him what I knew about my own body. At first I was hesitant. I wanted to let him take the lead, but as time went on, I knew that things in the bedroom could be better for me, and I so wanted that. I summoned the courage to take him on what I called a "pussy tour." I felt nervous, but also curious. I talked him through what I had learned about what I liked and what my body was capable of, creating a sweet, explorative atmosphere with him. He was a willing student, and it didn't take long for him to learn how to touch the deepest place of pleasure

within me. Now we tease each other sometimes, saying "more practice necessary!"

When it comes to practice, there is no one in the
world who knows your body as well as you do. No
one knows what your orgasms feel like or the best
way to help you become aroused or achieve orgasm.
Take the time to learn these things for yourself, and
be open to practicing how to perfect them alone and
with your partner.

Practice is a good place to bring in what we
talked about earlier in this chapter: creativity, curiosity, and play. Don't be afraid to be creative and
playful here, setting aside any domestications that
may prevent you from trying new things because of
old tapes or ideas. Some people think sex should be
serious all the time, so they maintain a certain mood,
but being creative and playful are simply more colors in your rainbow of sexual passion and joy.

One way to be creative and playful is to practice
exclusive giving and exclusive receiving. This is ini-
tially an uncomfortable challenge for some couples,
especially if one of you is used to being the giver and
the other the receiver. Try switching those roles for
a few encounters and see how it feels. For you givers,

notice what it is like to really lie back and exclusively receive pleasure. For you receivers, how does it feel when you are giving only during an encounter?

Practice completely, fully receiving, without any pressures to give back. Be playful in this encounter, and be comfortable that this session is just for you. When it's your partner's turn to be the receiver, practice giving fully. Listen to your partner's body with all of your senses. Try new touch, new pressure, new areas of sensitivity. Put all of your attention on your partner, not expecting anything in return. If they are an instrument, how do they want to be played?

And remember, practice makes perfect, so have fun and keep practicing!

The Emotional Connection

So far we have talked about the mind's role in our sexual encounters, but it's also true that your emotions play a big part in helping you feel connected to your partner. For instance, if you are holding on to any resentment, fear, or silent anger, these can shut down your sense of desire.

When we engage in sex from this state of mind, it often results in what we call surface sex—where your bodies come together on the surface but you keep any issues between you packed up in an inner suitcase for later. It goes without saying that while it may feel good in the moment, sex on this level will not fill your deepest yearnings to be seen and met by another. Again, if we are shutting down our willingness to experience pain or difficulty, we are also limiting our access to joy.

If there are any issues that you and your partner need to talk about, in most cases we advise diving into those before sex. Talking can help you clear any emotions or difficulty that can preoccupy you during sexual activity. The best sex can often occur when we drop our guard, allow ourselves to be vulnerable, and share any immediate emotions that we are in danger of shoving down inside of us.

In addition, sexual pleasure can sometimes bring up memories from the past, including old pain and emotions, even emotions where the source is a mystery to us. It's important not to suppress those emotions but to let them out. A friend of ours describes it this way:

When I first started being sexual as a young woman, I remember there was a point where right after I would orgasm I would have a complete meltdown. I would cry, and there were tears and snot . . . the whole thing. I don't know where those feelings came from, so I just shut them down, and this made me not want to have sex.

We can give each other permission to stay present with any grief or hurt or trauma that comes up before, during, or after sex. If this happens, let your partner know what's going on with you, and tell them it's not their fault or their job to fix it. Just ask them to be with you as you process and heal from these emotions that arise. It is only with your willingness—your gentle, compassionate, tender willingness—to open up to your vulnerability and share your hurts that deep healing and holding can happen.

Of course, this gets even more challenging for those who have been the victims of sexual assault. So much of our wounding and the accompanying emotions can become exposed during sex. Be gentle with yourself in these moments, and remember to seek the help of a counselor or recovery group to help you process them. This is a difficult journey, but the good news is that we have known many people who have been abused and have gone on to have healthy and happy sexual relationships with someone they love.

Attraction to Others

In our workshops and teaching sessions we are sometimes approached by people who are feeling sexual attraction to a person outside of their relationship, and they are afraid that means their relationship with their current partner is in trouble, or they feel guilty and think something is wrong with them.

If you're finding yourself attracted to others, our first recommendation is to not judge yourself or close yourself down. Instead, see this attraction as energy moving through you that you don't have to take any action on. When you see it as energy, you can then choose how you want to channel it: you can take it and put it toward your creativity in other areas, and you can channel that energy toward your relationship. In fact, we have found that attraction is often the result of wanting to create something new.

Rather than manufacture stress about your attraction to another or use it against yourself, we invite you to investigate the underlying cause of this energy. When you feel this energy of attraction, ask yourself what you are really craving, and see if there is a way you can give it to yourself, or something your partner can do to satisfy that craving. Oftentimes what appears to be a sexual attraction to others isn't really about sex, but something else that you're missing or craving, such as a deeper emotional connection, some focused attention, or increased physical tenderness.

For example, we have a friend who felt attracted to one of the dads from her son's school. She saw him many days at pickup and drop-off and admired how involved he was with his kids. They would talk from time to time, and she began to feel a physical attraction to him, even though both she and he were married. She didn't understand this attraction at first, but then it occurred to her that what she found so attractive was the way he was with his children. Her husband had been working a lot lately, and she was missing his involvement in the lives of their own children. Once she was able to identify the energy she was craving, she was able to go back to her husband and tell him that she missed his presence in the family. This paved the way for them to consciously create together. Looking back, our friend was deeply grateful for the message she got from her attraction and for the opportunity to return that energy to her partnership and family.

Our friend's story is a good example of how investigating the source of her attraction to another led her to find what she was really craving more of, and it wasn't really about sex at all. That's why we say it's important to explore what's underneath this energy rather than repress it through feeling guilty about it or wishing it wasn't there. If you repress them, your sexual attractions to others are more likely to spin out of control, because anytime you repress something, it tries to find a way to escape.

For instance, our friend who was attracted to the dad at school also explained to us that before she realized the underlying cause of her craving, she found that she would suppress the energy of her craving, and she noticed how this resulted in her being very critical of her husband. Then she finally recognized that the reason she was so critical of her husband was because she felt guilty about her attraction to someone else. When she investigated the energy, that's when she found the source of what she was really craving and was able to express that to her husband. The internal criticism stopped as a result, because she was no longer suppressing that energy.

In closing this chapter, we want to be clear that joy isn't an emotion reserved exclusively for special occasions like births and marriages—joy is an ongoing practice, particularly as it relates to relationships. It takes work sometimes to be joyous in a relationship and to keep that joy strong through the months and years as a relationship develops, grows, and changes. When you find your relationship in a rut or feeling stale, return to the sensation of joy that you knew early on in your partnership with your beloved; invest some time in creativity, play, and sex, and allow yourself to use these tools to transform the intimate connection between you and your beloved.

Explorations
Make Your Lists
Here is a set of four very important lists we would like you to make in order to foster passion and joy in your relationship:

1. Make a list of creative things you would like to try with your partner. Include some completely new things as well as ideas for doing old things in new ways. Examples: attend a creative class; paint each other's

portraits; build birdhouses together; garden; paint murals; make mud sculptures in the backyard; take horseback riding lessons; try the flying trapeze; study a foreign language in preparation for a trip; take meditation classes; volunteer together with elders, kids, animals, or those suffering from homelessness.

2. Make a list of fun things you would like to do with your partner. Remember, in most cases these activites should be solely for fun and not to accomplish anything. Notice if you have a tendency to combine fun with "getting something done," as the latter can sometimes interrupt the former. Examples: fishing or boating, golf or Frisbee golf, a night of dancing, strolling through a new neighborhood at dusk, wine tasting, seeing a play or concert, going on a hot air balloon ride.

3. Make a list of things that turn you on sexually in your life now (not what turned you on five months or five years ago). Get

still and investigate this idea with some real curiosity, and remember to have fun with it. One of our friends, who is a stay-at-home mom, said she gets sexually turned on when her husband helps her with the dishes and other household responsibilities! Be open to what really is sexy to you versus what your domesticated ideas tell you is "right" or "wrong." For instance, it might be the idea of having sex outside, or the taste of strawberries, or the sound of the rain. Open your senses again and ask yourself, "What turns me on now?"

4. Make a list of things you would like to try creatively and playfully when it comes to sex. Maybe it's taking a bath or shower together, being outside in the wilderness, or having sex after getting dressed up and having a night out on the town. Maybe it's role-playing, watching or reading something arousing together, doing a guided tour of each other's bodies, or practicing new massage or deep breathing techniques. Sexual experimentation, whether it's within the

container of a relationship or as a pathway to explore your own sexuality, can open you up to expanded sensations and new ways of perceiving sensuality and pleasure.

Next comes the important part, which may feel a little scary: share these four lists with your partner, and ask them to write their own lists and share them with you. You may be surprised by some of the things they put on their list, and they may be surprised by yours. If your partner doesn't want to make lists, you can still provide them with yours.

Making Dates for Creativity, Curiosity, Play, and Sex

One thing we know about rekindling the passion and joy in your relationship is that it's not enough to just want to make a change or even have the knowledge of what it takes to change; you have to *put that knowledge into action* to realize the benefits.

To that aim, look at your sets of lists and schedule dates to be creative, curious, playful, and sexual based on what you wrote. Set that time aside on your calendar, and then make it sacred. Combining and taking action on the work you have done here are what can really stoke the fires of passion and joy in your relationship.

You can plan ahead and say, "on our sex date, let's practice giving/receiving and that's it." Or you can have sex dates over a dinner out—and enjoy all the conversation and the mental and emotional aspects of exploring your sex as you eat in a public place. Play. Explore.

Remember: the willingness to take risks that combine vulnerability and creativity will take your relationship to a deeper level in record time.

Chapter 6

The Secret of Communication

Vulnerability is the only authentic state. Being vulnerable means being open, for wounding, but also for pleasure. Being open to the wounds of life means also being open to the bounty and beauty. Don't mask or deny your vulnerability: it is your greatest asset.

—Stephen Russell

Of all human activities, none has transformed our world more than communication. We humans have created magic together through things like art, music, architecture, and technology, just to name a few areas, and the spoken and written word were necessary for these achievements. While communication is perhaps one of the most important human tools, when it comes to intimate relationships, it's surprising how many of us struggle to communicate in healthy, productive ways.

Sure, most of us are able to communicate with our partners effectively when it comes to things we agree about or that we share in common—especially when the relationship is new and we are hanging on each other's every word. In many cases, being "someone we could really talk to" led us to choose one another in the first place. But as the relationship matures, many couples find they need deeper communication skills to connect with each other in the midst of issues or topics that challenge or even divide them.

Because of this, communication is the next transformative secret to a happy and healthy relationship. In our experience, effective communication comes much easier if you are practicing the lessons that have come before this one. In other words, the best communication occurs when both partners are grounded in commitment and freedom, have awareness of their own strengths and weaknesses, are healing themselves from unhelpful ideas and past emotional wounds, and are willing to work creatively to develop joy in their relationship, which includes finding creative solutions to disagreements when they arise.

The five previous practices can help your communication skills mature, but the transformative power of communication in relationships also includes something else: the willingness to be *vulnerable*.

Vulnerability in communication occurs when you share your wants, needs, and fears openly and honestly. Just as important, it entails actively remaining open as you listen to your partner's wants, needs, and fears in return. When both partners are vulnerable, you are better able to hear and respond to each other in a loving, connected, and helpful way. Vulnerability in communication includes the desire to find common ground, to be supportive, and to extend compassion in the process.

What does this type of vulnerability look like in action? For starters, it means you are willing to admit when you don't know, when you are wrong, or when you are scared. It often includes a plea for help, for understanding, and for love, all with an open heart. We won't sugarcoat it—practicing vulnerability can be very difficult. However, we have found that vulnerability's bark is much worse that its bite. That is, the voice in your head will defend to the death your right and responsibility to wear a protective suit of armor—"You can't tell them that!" it will shout—but once you muster the courage to lay aside that armor, you will very quickly see the gifts of remaining open and soft to your experience and your partner's.

A longtime student of ours described a vulnerable experience in her communication this way:

> The first time I really understood the power of vulnerability was during a conversation with a partner who was furious with me. Normally I would have placated them, run away, or gone completely numb.
>
> But then I remembered what you told me, so I decided to really listen to their upset. I felt my heart open and connect with their hurt. I didn't try to fix or change or defend. I witnessed the places my partner was speaking truth, and also the places they had made assumptions. I listened fully until they were finished, and then I noticed that I felt soft, undefended, and ready to share my truth.
>
> I was vulnerable.
>
> I took responsibility and apologized for my part of the miscommunication that had

sparked their upset. I shared my point of view and explained where I was afraid and what I wanted to happen next. My calm was contagious, and soon we finished the conversation, hugged, and went about our day feeling more connected to each other. This was a profound change from my previous defense mechanisms.

In this situation, our student chose vulnerability over its opposite, what we call "closing off." When we choose to close off in our communication instead of staying vulnerable, this can manifest in a variety of ways.

First, we may close off by pretending that everything is okay. We tend to do this if we are afraid our partners won't like what we have to say, or because we are afraid of being abandoned, or because we don't think it's worth the trouble to speak the truth. Our fear or apathy motivates us to go along with what is happening, and while we may smile on the outside, we might be building up resentment on the inside.

When we habitually go against our own desires by doing what the other person wants, not rocking the boat, or staying quiet, we invite misery into our relationship. Even when this behavior helps avoid a difficult conversation in the short term, in the long run your relationship with yourself and your partner will suffer because you are not being truthful about how you really feel. When we remain quiet in order to keep others "happy" at the expense of our own truth, we trade our integrity for our partner's comfort. We also rob our partner of the chance to contribute to our real happiness in a healthy way.

Secondly, some of us choose to close off by isolating or retreating when things get challenging. This may feel a bit more truthful than pretending that everything is okay, but we still aren't communicating our fears and needs to our partners. Instead, we metaphorically head for the hills, putting emotional or physical distance between our partner and ourselves. Disengaging may seem helpful in the short run, but it is damaging in the long run because the issues of course don't go away by themselves, they just get buried, poised to come out later with more emotional poison than before. We want to emphasize that this avoidance behavior doesn't include a conscious decision to leave a volatile conversation to cool off and reflect, which as we have said earlier can be very helpful. The difference is in the intent with which you leave the communication and what you do with the time away.

Finally, some of us may close off by striking back with anger, projecting an illusion of power as we yell or scream in an attempt to get our point across. Ironically, the person who yells in relationships is often the one who doesn't feel heard. Of course, the yelling doesn't fix this, and in fact most often it has the opposite effect. When someone yells at you, how likely are you to really listen? If you or your partner has a propensity to yell, it will be enormously beneficial to develop a system of truly listening to each other in times of stress and disagreement. Listening is a whole other part of the communication process that we will delve into in depth a little later, but for now let's focus on the speaking/expression part of communication.

We know that being vulnerable is not easy, and yet the results of bringing that intent into our communication with our partner are amazing. It touches their softness and allows them to meet us in a place that, as the poet Rumi says, "is beyond right or wrong." The field of vulnerability makes deep communication possible.

We are often asked to describe what vulnerability looks like in practice, so here are some action words that reflect the qualities of being vulnerable in our communication versus some that reflect closing off

Vulnerable	Closed Off
Body relaxed, deep breathing, shoulders loose and palms open, ease in making eye contact	Body rigid or constricted, fast or irregular breathing, arms crossed, jaw clenched, eye contact difficult
Feeling unconditional love for your partner no matter what they are doing	Feeling conditional love, wanting your partner to change
Present in the moment	Thinking of past/future
Curious and asking open-ended questions	Judgmental and making accusations
Compassionate	Angry
Listening intently	Projecting what you will say next

or the opposite of being vulnerable. You can use this as a checklist to become aware of your habits as you increase your capacity to stay soft and open.

Now, for those of you who are reading this list and saying to yourself, *Yes! My partner is closed off, that is what is wrong in our relationship!* we want you to take a big breath and remember what our goal has been throughout this entire process. Don't try to fix, force, or fight your partner so that they will change. This is not your job, nor is it within your power. Your job, your goal for this entire journey, is to learn to gently unfold and open, even to your partner's closure, and to keep finding the places within you that you are still closing off.

Maybe you are reading this and judging yourself because you recognize that you are closed off on a variety of topics. If so, take a big breath and be compassionate with yourself. Remember you are in the process of learning and growing, and that takes time and patience. You are on your way.

To ease the process of bringing vulnerability to your communication, especially as you first start on this phase of your journey, we have broken the steps to healthy communication down into the three main categories: listening, speaking, and silence.

Listening

When we think of communication, our minds typically run to the ways in which we can speak effectively. Rarely do we think of listening as the most important step. But our communication is only as good as our willingness to listen to our partners, and that is the very first step.

When you are listening with vulnerability, you are practicing conscious listening. This means you focus on hearing and understanding exactly what the other person is saying in the current moment. You aren't on your phone, or thinking about what you are doing later, or planning what you are going to say next. You are also listening without predicting what the other person is going to say, imagining you know the subtext underneath their words, or holding on to what they have said in the past and what you think you know about them. In short, you are bringing the attitude of "beginner's mind" (or the open, unbiased mind of a someone who is ready to learn, rather than the knowledge-filled mind of someone who knows all the answers) to your listening.

Conscious listening becomes more challenging when your partner says things you don't like or agree with. In these moments, through this listening practice, notice any discomfort you feel and try to lean into the situation and listen even more to what your partner is saying. If you are feeling defensive, try thanking this voice in your head for its input and its desire to protect you. This acknowledges the voice and its purpose without forcing you to attach to the ideas it is presenting. You can think to yourself, "Thank you for coming to my defense, but I don't need your help in this moment. I am staying open to these difficult emotions and listening to my partner right now." This allows you stay focused on what your partner is saying, rather than dismissing it in your head, or judging it, or immediately thinking of your point of view.

When you are consciously listening, you can ask your partner open-ended questions to help them express themselves more clearly, which will help you better understand them. It also can help to label the emotions involved. Look at the difference between these statements and questions (*see the chart on the following page*).

When both partners are listening and being vulnerable, then the communication can help take the relationship to a deeper level. A friend of ours shares this experience:

Emotionally Reactive Communication	Clear Emotional Communication
Are you serious? What were you thinking?	This is really hard, and I'm fighting against my instincts to run away and hide. How are you feeling right now?
Why would you ever do that? I don't get you.	You must have been really upset to have done that. Can you help me understand your thought process?
What's wrong with you? You're being ridiculous.	I'm really confused and frustrated. Is there something I am missing that you can fill me in on?

When issues come up that we don't agree on, I have a tendency to try to avoid conflict, and my partner has a tendency to push for conflict. When the topic of marriage came up again the other day, which is something that we don't agree on, I knew we had a choice. We could either go deeper in our communication with one another, or we could revert to our usual unhealthy patterns.

What ended up happening was that I got clear about my fears and the needs I had around wanting to get married, and I shared them with her. Her response was kind, she said she did not want me to be afraid, but at the same time she was unable to meet my needs right now. At first my feelings got hurt and I watched myself start to shut down, but then I remembered the importance of extending freedom to my partner, as I do want her to be free. This led to an honest discussion about what we both wanted from the relationship and to discovering the source of the issue or that we see things differently in this particular area. I want us to get married, and she views the institution of marriage as archaic and patriarchal. From here, we both shared what we were able to do and what we were not able to do around this issue, and we did so from a vulnerable place. We aren't in agreement on this issue, but we understand and respect each other's position, and it no longer leads to outright fighting as a result.

To be able to listen to your partner's fears and needs is the first step. However, as our friend's example shows, just because you listen to your partner and they listen to you doesn't mean you will find agreement on whatever the issue is. But when we truly listen to one another, we make room for creative solutions, compromises, and at the very least a level of understanding that can bring the end of a war.

Speaking

Speaking is what we think of most when it comes to communication, and learning to speak with vulnerability is key to maintaining peace in our relationships. This includes what for many of us is the most difficult part: speaking our truth with an open heart, even when our partners might not agree with or like what we have to say.

Many of us were never taught this skill, and it's not something that we tend to value highly in our society. Instead, we are told to "not say too much," or "don't expose yourself" when sharing, and that's if we are taught the practice of sharing our feelings at all. For many of us, attempts to share or open up have led to us being shamed or shut down. Men might have been told to "man up." Most of us missed the "this is how you share your feelings" class growing up.

Before we talk about speech in regard to speaking to another, we want to point out that vulnerable speech begins with noticing the way you speak to yourself. The voices of the judge and the victim we covered previously are some of the ways we mask vulnerability, and for most of us breaking up with these voices is an ongoing process. Notice when you berate yourself, or scold yourself, or ask yourself loaded questions like "Why did I do that again?" or "This relationship isn't working. What's wrong with me?" The judge and victim voices will be your cue to pay attention to what is going on and to become aware of how you are speaking to yourself.

The next time you notice yourself asking loaded questions, which carry inherent judgment and fear, take a step back to reorient yourself toward developing vulnerable speech. In any moment of sadness, anger, stress, fear, or other emotion that would lead you to close off rather than be vulnerable, we invite you to ask yourself the following:

- What am I afraid of in this situation?

- What is it that I want to happen now?

As you consider these questions, take a deep breath and close your eyes. Get really quiet and listen to your inner wisdom for the answers. This simple process allows you to start by being vulnerable with yourself, and when you find the answers to these questions, you can bring that same vulnerability and connection to speaking your truth to your partner. Let this be an alternative to closing off and reacting in an unhelpful way—you might be surprised at the result.

For instance, Jen, a student of ours, had some past experiences that left her with a substantial amount of emotional trauma. As a child, she witnessed a lot of verbal and physical abuse between her parents, and as a result she would often shut down and go numb anytime her partner raised his voice during an argument. As Jen became aware of this and began to heal herself from this old pain, she also needed to share her truth with her partner so he could better understand the situation. She asked herself those two questions, and then once she was clear on the answers, she shared them with her part-ner. Here's an example of her part of the dialogue:

> When we are having a disagreement and you raise your voice, I get very scared, and my tendency is to shut down. This is because it reminds me of when I was a child and I witnessed all the verbal and physical abuse between my parents. I know you would never hurt me, but if you could do your best to speak to me in a calm voice instead, I feel like I would better be able to hear you and stay engaged in the conversation.

Once Jen's partner heard it explained this way, he became more conscious of his own speech and did his best to honor her request. When she asked herself what she was afraid of, she was able to iden-tify the childhood fears that were being brought up in her present circumstance. She was also able to consider with an open heart that she was afraid to share her feelings with her beloved. Would he understand? Would he reject her feelings? Would he think she was being ridiculous? It took some bravery to go against her hiding instincts and share how she felt. And that wasn't all. She went further, calmly relaying her answer to the second question, What do I want? From a place of vulnerability, she was able to make a request about what she wanted to happen. In this case, Jen's partner was able to meet her request, but of course that won't always happen. Even in more difficult situations, when we are able to listen and speak vulnerably to one another, we leave space for other creative solutions to emerge.

When we hold back our truth in stressful or uncomfortable situations, we are prolonging the inevitable, as the issues at hand don't go away; they just go underground and come back later with more intensity.

Poor Speech Habits

Many of us never learned a good practice of speaking with vulnerability, and instead we often pick up and rely on what we call "poor speech habits." Let's look at a few of the most common forms of these habits—using words as weapons, passive-aggressive communication, clamming up, and saying yes when you mean no—and see how they are quite opposite to vulnerability.

WORDS AS WEAPONS

In a way, words can be like knives in your relationship. On the one hand, wielded skillfully, they can be as precise and as effective as a surgeon's scalpel, or even the everyday kitchen utensil, carefully used to prep nourishing meals. But when wielded unskillfully, words can be like daggers in the heart, resulting in pain, hemorrhaging, and even death of the relationship.

Any word will transform into a weapon the moment we use it with the intent to create pain in another person. Rather than sharing our truth with vulnerability, we often use our words to attack character, change the subject by adding accusations of our own, or bring up a past hurt. When past hurts come into play, true communication about the current situation has stopped, because now you're no longer in the present moment, you're immersed in something that happened five days or five years ago. Adding insults or accusations or bringing up the past are means to put your partner on the defensive so you can "win" the argument or discussion. In truth, of course, no one wins.

Take the example of our friends Josephine and Beth. After years of struggling financially, they finally came into a place of being able to save up for a down payment on a home. Even though they agreed on their goals and methods, they continued to clash about shared expenses and little luxuries. Finally, Beth decided to ask herself the two questions: "What am I afraid of?" and "What is it that I want to happen now?" With these responses, she was able to come to Josephine with an open heart.

As it turned out, Beth was holding on to a past hurt in their relationship, a time when Josephine's overspending brought them to the edge of bankruptcy. While they had worked through much of this together, Beth found she would still bring it up in their arguments, claiming she couldn't trust Josephine. With a little digging and a little bravery, Beth realized it wasn't fair to bring up past hurts in this way, but that she *could* talk about her current level of trust. After all, this was the answer to her second question: "I want to trust that we are on the same page with our goals." Then, with vulnerability, she could share this with Josephine about her present feelings:

We have come a long way together around money issues, and I am still rebuilding trust with you and with myself about our past spending habits. I promise to work on not bringing up old hurts to try to make my points in the present. I am hoping that you can help me by taking extra time each month to go through our finances with an open heart and keep the communication channels open for ways we can both stay on track.

As a result, Josephine was better able to understand where Beth was coming from. And the two of them even decided to make a fun monthly at-home dinner occasion out of their shared goal of reviewing their finances. Had Beth not taken the time to consider her fears and her wants and articulate them to her partner, they might have stayed stuck in their old patterns of talking about past wounds around money.

Sometimes we use words as weapons in subconscious ways, and here is where the practice of awareness can really help. For instance, if you are disagreeing on a consequence for your child, you might be tempted to bring in your partner's sister and her discipline practices with her own children. While saying something like, "You're just like your sister," or "This is what your sister does with her kids," might appear harmless, it really has nothing to do with the situation between the two of you. Instead, you have clouded the issue and subtly attacked your partner by inference. Thankfully, developing our awareness can help us notice the little ways we can poison the waters between us without even intending it.

Rather than using your words as weapons, come back to the two questions: What am I afraid of in this situation? and What is it that I want to happen now? Staying focused on these questions can help you choose words that express how you feel, explore why you feel that way, and determine what can make you feel better. This is what opens the door for true communication to take place.

PASSIVE-AGGRESSIVE COMMUNICATION

Passive-aggressive communication occurs when we don't express how we really feel, but rather pretend to be okay with a situation, pushing our fears and true desires down. In this way, we make a beeline for feeling resentful at our partner and even striking back at them as a result. This kind of exchange can also contain the seed of conscious or unconscious manipulation as we try to steer our partner to guessing that our actual wants and needs are different than the ones we are communicating.

When we discussed the secret of freedom in lesson two, we wrote about Joe and Mary, and how they had dinner plans at Joe's parents that Mary wanted to opt out of at the last minute to be with her friends instead. When Mary asked Joe if this was okay, he said that it was, but that's not how he really felt. When she got home later that evening, he was cold and reserved, punishing her by withholding his love and affection, all the while saying everything was fine.

Had Joe instead chosen to speak vulnerably, the conversation may have gone something like this:

> *Mary:* "I know we have plans with your parents tonight, but my friends have an extra ticket to the opera. Do you mind if I go with them instead?"

> *Joe:* "Well, I'm feeling torn on this. I really wanted you to come to dinner with my family, it's important to me, and I will be disappointed if you can't make it. At the

same time I want you to do what you really want to do, so let's talk about it more. Is going to the opera really important to you? How do you feel about it?"

By responding this way, Joe has opened the door for true communication to take place.

If you notice, Joe shared how he felt and then asked his partner for more information. Passive-aggressive communication is often based on a need for control that comes from a fear that we will not get what we want or need from our partner—that we have to engineer it ourselves. We can make a braver and more vulnerable choice: to entrust our wants and needs to the shared actions within our partnership. We do this by not only sharing how we feel but also inviting our partner to have a conversation about the issue in hopes of finding a solution that works for both of us.

CLAMMING UP

The next poor speech habit is one of omission rather than commission. In other words, what we don't say can cause as much trouble as what we do. For instance, some of us have been domesticated to believe that if our partners love us, they will just know what we want or need. But this simply isn't true, or fair, as our partners are not mind readers. Even if our partner shows that they can be very intuitive to our wants and needs, no one can be expected do this perfectly all the time.

You can remedy this by committing to share with your partner what you would like to happen. For instance, we know two people, Stevie and Aliyah, who have been in a relationship for many years. For Aliyah, the anniversary of the relationship is something she really likes to celebrate with dinner, dancing—the works. Stevie, on the other hand, was unaware of her desire and would often let the day pass without too much fanfare. For the first couple of years they were together, Aliyah stayed quiet and hoped Stevie would surprise her. When this didn't happen, she would get sad, frustrated, or even mad, thinking that Stevie "should know" this was important to her. Finally, when she shared how she felt about the situation and what she wanted to happen instead, Stevie smiled good-naturedly and said, "I had no idea that you wanted to celebrate this way. Let's do it!" Problem solved.

SAYING YES WHEN YOU MEAN NO

Finally, a common way couples create discomfort and even resentment in a relationship is to say yes when they really mean no. While we all want to exercise the spirit of compromise in many areas with our beloved, if your partner asks you to do something and you say yes when deep down you really mean no, then you are setting yourself up for trouble. Furthermore, if you aren't careful, you might come to blame your partner for the resulting undesired outcome, rather than realizing that the error was yours and not theirs. Remember, commitment to you means that sometimes you say no to your partner from a place of love rather than saying yes from a place of accommodation. It's okay to say no to others in order to say yes to yourself.

The Written Word

Before we move on to silence, let us take a moment to address vulnerability and the written word. Writing is another way that we can use words to communicate our truth from the heart. Sometimes writing down your thoughts, especially the answers to the two questions we mentioned earlier, can be a useful tool in preparing to have an important conversation.

In this way, the written word can help you make a plan for what you want to say in an important conversation. After you've written out your plan, let it sit for a day or two, and then revisit it. Feel free to edit and adjust after you've had time to reflect. Once you are at peace with what's on the page, use these talking points as a guide to have that conversation.

Another way to use the written word is to write your beloved a letter. Here, too, you can reflect for a day or two on what you say prior to delivering your message. This can be a good tool if you feel your partner is unable to hear you or let you finish in a particular situation, but be sure to check yourself and confirm that you are willing to listen to their response and that you aren't using this method to avoid having to face their reply. In our view, writing to your partner, used sparingly, can be a good precursor to face-to-face communication in certain situations. Of course, there is no substitute for presence.

Silence

While the spoken word is the most common way we communicate, we can also send powerful, complex messages through our silence as well. We may think of silence in a relationship context as mostly negative, as a means of avoidance or as a way to show our dissatisfaction. As playwright George Bernard Shaw wrote, "silence is the most perfect expression of scorn." Silence in this regard is rarely a hallmark of vulnerability.

On the other hand, if our intentions are to bring healing and peace to the relationship, silence can be a wonderful tool in communication. Many times when our partners are fearful or upset, the most helpful thing we can do is listen and, rather than respond, simply maintain a silent presence with them. Sometimes our partners just need to vent; they don't need our advice or for us to say anything. We can also provide a kind of mirror for our partners in this situation with simple, calm statements that name and reflect the feelings our partner is expressing. If they're fed up with a coworker, we can mirror back with a phrase like, "that sounds really frustrating." Even simple phrases like "I see," "aha," or "uh-huh" can offer an empathetic response that supports your partner without adding your own point of view or opinions to the mix.

As self-help teachers and authors, we find we need to practice this in our own relationships with regularity. In other words, when students and readers come to us with their relationship issues and questions, part of our job is to make a suggestion, give an answer, or share our own experience. But this is not the case with our own partners, and so we are mindful that we only give our opinion when requested. What we have found in discussing this with couples is that they often feel that way too, and that there are certain times they just need a listening ear and some love. We have included an exercise that can make this a fun game at the end of the chapter.

Another helpful place to practice silence in your relationship is when you drop the need to point out that you are right in a situation or you realize you don't need to have the last word in a discussion. We have noticed that it is quite natural for some people to want to have the last word even when they may think it's not important to them. This practice of letting go of having the last word is simple enough, but you must remember to practice it. As you are in the midst of a conversation, hold off on an impulse to say the last thing. Allow your partner to finish their thought, and then just breathe and hold space for the talk to come to a close. If this feels difficult to you, remember that many of us don't recognize this habit within ourselves, and we can all practice letting go of the last word.

Finally, sitting silently with your partner, with both of you saying nothing, is a kind of mediation in and of itself. In this place of pure being, neither of you needs to fill the space with words or actions. This practice is particularly special when you try it with someone you love, but it is also wonderful to practice by yourself as well.

Communication in Conflict

While we have covered listening, speaking, and silence separately, in action they of course happen interchangeably, depending on the nature and specifics of the situation. Vulnerable communication tools are often needed most when emotions are running high, the very times when being open and remembering our budding skills can be most challenging. In our view, getting better at our communication is a lifelong process, not something that will ever be fully accomplished.

Before moving on, we'd like to say a little more about conflict, because that is where our vulnerable communication is needed the most. Disagreements can actually be very healthy for a relationship—*even when they can't be resolved.* Conflict is a natural part of any relationship, and as we indicated early on, not experiencing much of it isn't always a sign that everything is good in the relationship. Even when conflicts can't be resolved, they can still result in bringing us closer as the energy of the argument is transformed through curiosity, connection, and trust. To start, we must notice how we treat our partner and ourselves when disagreements come up.

When you approach a disagreement from the position of "I am right" and don't take the time to really listen to your partner, you will face difficulty. Everyone wants and deserves to be heard. Some of you reading this may be feeling like you are unheard in your own relationship, and you may be right; but oftentimes the way to get your partner to really listen to you is to go deeper in *your* listening to them. Once you have done this, and they can really see that you have listened, you can ask that you too be heard.

Disagreements and conflict can actually deepen your relationship if both parties are willing to engage honestly. See your disagreements as an opportunity to practice awareness and healing. In the midst of friction, stop for a moment and ask yourself, "Is the position I am taking in this disagreement based on domesticated ideas or past wounds? Am I experiencing any fear as a result of the disagreement? How reasonable or realistic is that fear?" The fear list you made earlier can come in handy here.

The communication methods we choose are often indicative of how we will handle the disagreement. If we are able to name our fears and wants with vulnerability, this shows a willingness to work toward a solution agreeable to both parties. We can then use this conflict to choose to go deeper with each other. Setting aside the power dynamics of "winning" the argument or "being right," you might even reach the understanding that this is something you simply don't agree on, and then you can give each other any needed space in this area.

If we close off, revert to yelling or acting out, or pretend to agree to keep the peace, we know that we have more work to do around this area of conflict. Rather than beat yourself up when and if you take one of these routes during a disagreement, simply notice it, ask yourself what part of your thinking needs to be investigated and healed, and envision how you can do better in the communication the next time.

Finally, we want to remind you that just because you communicate effectively with your partner, it doesn't mean you will always find agreement on the issue at hand. When you don't, the best alternative in these situations is that you "respectfully disagree" with each other, which means you really have listened to your partner, spoken your truth, and come to a place of acceptance on each other's point of view. Even if a conflict is unresolved, going through a process of vulnerable communication takes much of the sting and energy out of it and deepens your relationship at the same time.

The Richness of Communication

We want to be clear that communication isn't only a tool to solve problems; it is also a paintbrush that helps create the beautiful work of art that is your relationship. In this regard, sharing positive communication on a regular basis is key to helping your relationship thrive. Saying "I love you," "I see you," and "I am grateful for you" adds brightly colored strokes to your shared canvas.

Sometimes we can get out of the habit of expressing these little things. This is when cultivating creativity and play when it comes to your communication can be particularly helpful. Set silly challenges for yourselves—write love notes and leave them on the bathroom mirror, create code words or emojis that you can text throughout the day, or even sing a song for a special occasion. Love is in the details and in the everyday ways we speak, shout, share, and whisper our feelings.

Explorations

Being Curious

Asking open-ended questions, of yourself and your partner, can really help deepen your conversations. Gently remind yourself to steer toward questions free from judgments or assumptions and avoid questions that cast blame or come preloaded with a negative bias. For instance, "Why do you always do that?" might seem true to you in the moment, but it can also put your partner on the defensive.

Having awareness of your intention behind a question is key. Are you genuinely curious and open to hearing the answer? Or do you already think you know the answer, and are instead looking to teach your partner a lesson or show them you are right?

The next time you and your partner are discussing a difficult issue, try seeking more knowledge by asking the following questions:

- How are you feeling at this very moment?

- What do you want to happen next?

- What is it that I can do to help in this situation?

Questions like these can help you and your partner when you approach them with genuine curiosity and remain open as you listen to the responses.

Saying No

Some of us have been so domesticated to be accommodating that we have trouble saying no. If this is you, this exercise can help.

First of all, ask yourself the following questions and really think about the answers:

- Is it okay for you to say no?

- Is it okay for you to create boundaries?

- Is it okay for you to say things your partner may not want to hear?

- Can you speak without taking responsibility for your partner's reactions?

- And can you do all of these things with your heart wide open?

In an ideal world, the answer to each of these questions is yes. If you had trouble with answering yes to any of them, we encourage you to write the affirmative answer to those questions, and try them on for size. Begin each sentence with "I am free to . . ." For example,

- I am free to say no to my partner.

- I am free to set boundaries with my partner.

- I am free to say things my partner might not want to hear.

- I am free to speak without taking responsibility for my partner's reactions to my words.

- I am free to speak with my heart wide open.

Notice how you feel after writing your affirmative statements. Remember, these affirmations don't run contrary to your desire to listen, engage, and even accommodate your partner when doing so feels good to you; they are instead designed to help you share your truth with vulnerability, and this includes saying no, creating boundaries, and saying things that may make your partner uncomfortable.

Sometimes the fear of no can dissipate with a little practice. If your partner is open to it, you can play this game together to loosen up your "no" muscles. Each of you can take turns asking each other to do outrageous things and responding with an emphatic negative. "Will you eat a worm?" "No!" "Can I have a million dollars?" "No way!" Who knows, you might even get an unexpected yes. "Want to run around the block?" "Yes!"

Vent, Advice, Share

Here is a simple game for couples that can help you know when to listen, speak, or be silent. You will be creating a signal so that you and your partner know the goal of the conversation. Start by stating your intention—vent, advice, or share—so your partner knows what's coming:

Vent: If one of us needs to vent and express our frustration after a hard day, we say, "Vent!" One person takes five minutes (set a timer) to vent as fully and dramatically as possible. Once those five minutes are up, we stop and move on.

Advice: If we want advice about the situation we are about to share, we say, "Advice!" so the other person knows to get their creative brain in gear.

Share: If we say, "Share!" that means "I'm really excited about something—I'm inviting you to cheerlead and celebrate with me!"

As with most games, it takes two willing participants. So after you say vent, advice, or share, the other person can say, "Give it to me!" or "Not now!" which means, "I don't have the space for communicating right now."

The Much-Needed Conversation

Is there a conversation that you need to have with your partner but have been afraid to initiate? Can you set a goal and make a plan to do this within the next two weeks? Start by answering the two questions we covered earlier in the chapter: What am I afraid of in this situation? and What is it that I want to happen now?

Next, continue by writing the main points you want to share. Set your writing aside for a day or two and return to it with fresh eyes. What else do you need to share with your partner regarding this situation? Use your written plan to have a vulnerable conversation with your partner about this issue.

Practice Your Opening Lines

How we begin a conversation can often determine how it will go. When we start by expressing ourselves with vulnerability, things typically go much *much* better. To this end, we can follow the model of "I feel this way about XYZ because _____." Here are some starting lines for a vulnerable conversation:

- I feel scared to bring this up because I am afraid you will reject me . . .

- I feel tender about this because it is something I have been holding on to for many years . . .

- I realized when I feel you are pulling away
  that I get angry and start lashing out,
  because I am terrified you are going to
  leave . . .

What are some other ways you can begin a conversation with vulnerability?

THE
NOURISHING
SECRET

Chapter 7

The Secret of Release

*Breathe. Let go. And remind yourself that this very
moment is the only one you know you have for sure.*
—Oprah Winfrey

We'd like to begin this final lesson with a story:

One day an old man saw someone walking
through the desert. He invited the traveler
into his home to dine and spend the night.
Of course, the fellow eagerly accepted the
hospitality.

However, as the old man was preparing
the meal, he learned that the traveler had
opposing views on politics and religion to

his own. The old man asked the traveler to leave without giving him so much as bread to eat.

That night, the old man's wife came to him and asked, "Why did you treat your guest so poorly?"

The old man replied, "Because he obstinately opposed my views on politics and God."

The wife said, "But, my husband, I have put up with your differences in opinion for eighty years. Couldn't you have endured him for one night?"[2]

As this humorous little tale suggests, one of the most challenging aspects of nourishing happy and healthy relationships is paradoxical, as it involves not doing rather than doing. This is what we refer to as the secret of release. In successful relationships there are hundreds of little releases, or instances of letting go, starting from the very beginnings of a budding relationship. In fact, we know that in order to grow

---

[2]Adapted from "The Patience of a Friend" in Todd Outcalt's *Candles in the Dark: A Treasury of the World's Most Inspiring Parables* (Hoboken, NJ: John Wiley & Sons, 2002), 99.

and build something new, we must actively release and even suffer the loss of our previous reality.

For instance, we start a partnership when we release being single. In monogamous relationships, this means we release ourselves from dating other potential partners. As our new relationship grows, we are also releasing the idea of total independence, as we are now accountable, at least in some basic areas, to another person. At the start of a new partnership, we tend to give these things up quite willingly in the excitement of new love.

The next round of releasing can prove more challenging. We might have to bring a bit more conscious effort to release things like the need to be right all the time, the need to have the last word, and the need to control our partner's behavior, whether overtly or through manipulation. While harder than the first round of releasing, these things are still just the beginning.

There is yet another kind of releasing that doesn't get much press in self-help books and circles, and we'd like to draw your attention to it. This special type of release can be summed up in this morning greeting: "Good morning, my love, who are you today?"

Now you may be saying to yourself, "Well, that's an odd question to ask! How does that help with releasing?" But you'll find that the key to letting go and releasing is to be curious about the present, rather than attached to the past. You see, to nourish a happy and healthy relationship over the long term, we want to continually release who our partner has been in the past in order to explore who they are now. This includes releasing any designs we have on who they will become. While releasing in this way can at first seem like a negative, in reality this practice is intensely positive and indeed something that all happy couples do over time, even if they don't name it as such.

Although you may not often think of it this way, the truth is that you, your partner, and everyone else in the world is changing every day. Sometimes these changes are trivial, sometimes they are momentous; but couples in happy and healthy relationships embrace this constant of change rather than fight it.

For instance, have you ever looked at a family photo album of a couple that has been together for many years? At the various stages in their lives, you may find a photo or two where one or both partners are unrecognizable to you. It seems impossible that the person you know is the same as this other version, wearing different clothes or sporting a funky hairdo. As you lean in closer, you may notice that some essentials have not changed, such as their eyes or a certain expression—all the way back to their baby pictures—even if so much else seems completely transformed. This is analogous to the inner changes that we all undergo throughout our lives. While our essential essence remains, so much about us is continuously transformed.

Many of us might be frightened by the thought that our partners are changing, because we have so much invested in who we know and want them to be: our love, our hopes, our financial security, our emotional comfort, our sense of family. How can we reconcile these things with an openness to change? To do so means we must embark on an internal balancing act. Imagine a tightrope walker with a long pole who finds that sweet space with the weight and length of these opposing forces. On one end, there is the changing roles, desires, needs, and fears of our partner and ourselves and, on the other end, our need for stability within the relationship. Just as the tightrope walker progresses in what looks like one fluid motion, you and your partner are in fact in a similar process of continuous input and adjustment, balancing and rebalancing.

In her book *Mating in Captivity*, Esther Perel speaks to this core tension in relationships between the desire for familiarity and comfort (attachment) and the desire for excitement and adventure (exploration). When we are first dating, in the flush of excitement, we yearn for stability and a known future. But when we have been in a relationship for a long time and are settled into our routines, we long for newness and mystery. This is the koan, or puzzle, of relationships: the dynamic tension between comfort and exploration, safety and freedom.

We can only begin to satisfy both sides of the equation when we let go of the false belief that our partner should be the same person they were yesterday or that we will be the same person we were yesterday. In place of this belief, we can embrace them and ourselves for the unknown people we are today. When we commit to release these past versions in a generous way, we trust that the dynamics and roles that each of us play in the relationship will shift over time. If we expect ourselves, our partners, or our life situations to stay the same for the course of the relationship, we are out of touch with reality.

The good news is that embracing this change, and being excited about it, is what can keep the fire burning in your relationship for years to come. When you realize that you and your partner are changing all the time, being together is a continuous adventure, as you sail off to discover new lands and possibilities.

In fact, we like to think that being in a long-term relationship is like sailing a boat on the open ocean. The weather, tides, and currents constantly change, demanding our attention and action. When a relationship is healthy and nourished, we feel safe in a way that allows us to face forward and navigate the many exciting (and sometimes fearful) challenges that lie before us on the vast waters. We do not grasp tightly to the sails in an effort to control the wind—that might capsize us. We also do not let the sails flap loose, as that would squander any forward momentum. Instead, we work together in a state of constant, dynamic, relaxed tension, reading the waves, the wind, and the needs of the boat while keeping an eye on the horizon.

When we get attached to an image of what our relationship should be, or what our partners should be, or what we should be, these images become anchors that keep our boat from sailing freely across the open seas. Sometimes the anchor that is the most difficult to let go of is the one that insists our partners should be something other than who they are right here, right now.

Think for a moment about any anchors in your relationship that you need to release. Are there ways in which you want or expect your partner to be different from how they actually are? Where do you want or expect yourself to be different? These are the attachments that are keeping you from sailing freely, and we invite you to release the weight.

The key to this type of releasing is to return, over and over again, to seeing your partner, yourself, and your journey together through the eyes of unconditional love, because every attachment you have is really just a condition you have placed on yourself or your partner.

Seeing through the eyes of unconditional love can seem like a fluffy or nebulous suggestion, but in fact it is the most concrete way imaginable to practice the secret of release. The truth is that seeing and loving with conditions create far more complications than seeing and loving unconditionally. Like the paradox we mentioned at the start of this chapter, the idea of doing by not doing, seeing your partner through unconditional love pulls away the veil so you don't have to do all the work of creating and maintaining conditions. When you see your partner with your mental checklist active—including what they should be doing, thinking, or feeling—you know in that moment that you've moved away from unconditional love. It may not be easy, but you have a choice to see your partner through the eyes of unconditional love, not wanting them to be any other way than how they are in this moment.

This doesn't mean you don't set boundaries, and you will of course continue to experience the human emotions of sadness, anger, fear, and the like. You may even have to say goodbye sometimes. But all of this can occur with unconditional love as the backdrop. That is a beautiful thing about being human—we have the ability to experience complex emotions, some positive and some negative, often simultaneously.

Just as we explored in the secret of communication, the practice of releasing through unconditional love comes much easier when you are practicing the other lessons of healthy and happy relationships. In fact, every lesson in this book is actually a prescription for exactly how you can extend unconditional love to your partner and yourself.

When you are committed to finding and following your inner voice rather than your inner judge or victim; when you extend freedom to your partner to be who they are; when you become aware of your own domestications, attachments, and past traumas, as well as embrace a desire to heal yourself from them; and when you commit to cultivating joy in your relationship while communicating with vulnerability—then you are bringing unconditional love to your relationship through your actions.

Unconditional love can feel like a holy grail—an unattainable object we could search for our whole lives and never find. If we maintain this belief, we can look for it in all the wrong places, never realizing that unconditional love isn't a noun, it's a verb. You feel unconditional love only when you engage in the act of unconditionally loving.

When you choose to unconditionally love your partner as they are now, you are first feeding yourself the energy of love, and then this love energy will spill over to them. Loving in this way is what makes you feel good on the inside. Many people don't realize this, but you don't feel good as a result of your partner loving you; you feel good as a result of you loving them.

Like a cup running over, you can only give love when you have enough to fill you up. When you judge your partner, criticize them, or wish they were different, you are actually eating that negative energy yourself and blocking the feeling of love inside you. When you block the flow of unconditional love, you lay the groundwork for any problem you might experience with your partner (or anyone else, for that matter). Through the conscious practice of release, you can reopen the floodgates for love to pass through.

In these ways, releasing and unconditional love go hand in hand. In action it looks like this: you don't wish you or your partner were any different than how you both are right now. Sure, you may have preferences, but your preferences are no longer demands, and even when you and your partner do disagree on a particular issue, it is seen for its relative importance rather than becoming something artificially significant. Rather than getting upset by something insignificant that your partner says or does (such as leave the cap off the toothpaste or voice an opinion you disagree with), you find that these things no longer bother you all that much. In fact, you may simply giggle and see this thing you don't like as an endearing quality about your partner instead.

When you and your partner do disagree on something significant, you find that you are more open to coming up with a creative solution and can express how you feel with vulnerability.

Finally, when we release our reliance on conditional love, we can also let go of interacting with a fantasy version of someone we love. If our partner is exercising their freedom in a way that we wouldn't prefer but that we know is best for them, we might try asking ourselves, "Why is this better for me than what I originally wanted?" It's a tough question to ask in some cases, but the spirit of it means that we are looking for the hidden benefit to the situation and releasing our partner to follow their own path in the process.

When our loved ones are going through a hard time or behaving in ways we don't support, we tend to try to fix their problems or provide the help that *we* think they need. This kind of thinking can actually block the presence and creativity it takes to sit in the mud with a loved one, offer them unconditional love, and work out what's okay and what's not okay together. Remember, we cannot change another person. Only ourselves.

As anyone who has been in a relationship for a long time will tell you, there will be times when relationships earn the expression that they are "a lot of work." But here's yet another paradox: loving unconditionally is actually the easier and softer way to put in the work in a relationship—we only make it hard by holding on to our attachments rather than releasing them.

At the deepest level, there is no you or your partner, no HeatherAsh or Miguel, as we are all part of the One Life that is manifested in form. This deep truth resides in most every spiritual tradition: anything you do to another, you also do to yourself. Intimate relationships invite us to stretch ourselves to meet this truth and to release anything we hold against our partners, because we release ourselves in the process.

Trust and Release

Trust is the engine that drives effective release. A simple definition of trust is the idea of allowing something we care about to be vulnerable to the actions of others. When we release something, we are willing to accept a certain amount of vulnerability with the faith that we are pursuing the best possible outcome for all parties involved. Trust is the foundation for true intimacy in a relationship, as love flourishes where trust is planted and cultivated.

Indeed, when it comes to trusting your partner, you cannot trust that they will never do or say something that hurts you, or be insensitive, or communicate poorly. You can bet that, just like you, your partner is going to make mistakes. Remember, we are not trusting our partners to be a perfect fantasy version of themselves; we are trusting that they are doing their best and that they will learn from their mistakes. We will do the same. Our partners, like us, deserve to be loved and to give love along the way.

When you trust yourself, you release the idea that having trust for someone else can sustain you fully, because now you have your own back. You know that you can trust yourself to talk to your partner if they do something that hurts you, you can trust yourself to make boundaries, you can trust yourself to ask for what you need, and you can trust yourself to end the relationship if needed.

If you are struggling with trust in your relationship, take some time to review and discuss the agreements of your relationship with each other. Name what you want in the relationship, what your intent is, and what you want to bring to the partnership. Tell your partner exactly what you hope they will bring to the partnership, and ask questions of them if there is any confusion. Again, build your trust on who they are now, flaws and blessings all taken into account. Trust that they will be whoever they are, and remember to keep asking, "Who are you today?"

Trust flourishes when we feel seen, held with respect, and nourished. Listening deeply, cultivating connection, and maintaining presence in the moment are all skills. No one is magically born with them, and each and every one of us can practice and get better. When we feel we can be vulnerable and honest and not punish or judge our partner when they do the same, our armor softens and we let each other deeper into the process of cocreating our lives. Be sure to extend these actions to your partner as well as ask for them in return. This is how unconditional love unfolds.

When you are in a moment of darkness or uncertainty in a relationship, take comfort from the fact that trust actually grows the most when you go through difficult times together and come out the other side. Great relationships are not defined by the absence of conflict, disappointment, upset, or unplanned twists and turns. Like pottery, all great relationships go through a "firing" process that strengthens and beautifies them in the heat. If you share your truth, have compassion for your partner, stay present with any hurt, and continue to choose love, you'll come out on the other side of difficult situations more connected, open, and trusting of one another.

Death as a Release

Death, whether expected or sudden, is part of life, and there is no escaping it.

All relationships are guaranteed to end in the world of physical existence. Even if you and your partner spend decades together, at some point one of your bodies will cease all functioning. This is perhaps our most fundamental truth: our bodies age with each passing day, and all bodies are going to die.

When we bring that reality into our relationship, not in a spirit of fear, but rather knowing that every moment is precious, we can ask ourselves: "How do we want to use our time together?" This knowledge is an invitation to make every day with your partner precious. If this were your last day on the planet, you probably wouldn't hold on to the little things that irk or upset you. We'd guess that in fact whatever intimacy and vulnerability available to you would come forward and pour out.

In the Toltec tradition we bring to mind the image of the angel of death, not to generate fear, but rather as a symbol that reminds us of the fragility of life and the gift of experiencing it now. Too often we go through our daily lives pretending that nothing is ever going to happen to our bodies. In this way we can become complacent, take our relationships for granted, and think that we still have plenty of time to do what we most want to do or express how we feel to the ones we love.

The angel of death comes into our consciousness as a friend and ally, and it helps us bring that spark back into our lives. Through meditation on this image, we stop thinking, "Yeah, I have tons of time," and we admit, "I actually don't know how much time I have. No one does." At any moment, you or your partner could be gone. Meditating on this can actually benefit the relationship.

The angel of death reminds us that we have a choice: we can live each moment of our relationship in fear and attempts to control, or we can choose in each moment to live through the power of unconditional love and release. Nothing is "good" or "bad" unless we make it so. The most difficult situation can benefit your relationship, and the most minute thing can damage it. Even when we haven't chosen a situation, we get to choose our response. Everything dies, and every death offers the potential for transformation.

Releasing the Relationship

Lastly, there comes a time in some relationships when one or both partners no longer want to stay in the boat together. No one test or guideline will tell us if it is time to bring a relationship to a conscious close. There is only choice, and no choice can be right or wrong. It's simply a choice.

We encourage you to take your time with this decision and, at the same time, remain mindful that avoiding or postponing the end of a relationship can bring stagnation and suffering to both partners.

Sometimes endings are graceful, and sometimes they are not. When you come to the close of a relationship, you still get to choose how you navigate the ending. You can apply the same lessons for having a healthy, happy relationship to ending a relationship that is not healthy or happy: commit to yourself, free your partner, and communicate with vulnerability even as you release the relationship itself.

And remember, you can end the relationship with unconditional love. This can be extremely difficult, but it brings a sense of radical freedom to your being. We have a friend whose wife, after ten years of marriage, announced to him that she wanted a divorce, in part because she was in love with someone else. Our friend was heartbroken, and he gave a list of reasons why his wife shouldn't do this: "This breaks up our family, you made a promise, I can change your mind," and many more. But as he looked deeper into himself, he saw that he was actually placing all sorts of conditions on her to receive his love. This realization was wrenching for him, as letting go of those ideas meant he suffered an enormous loss of certainty as well as having to face the loss of his relationship. But he stayed with it and remained open to the painful experience. Ultimately, he went back to her and said, "I love you and I want you to be happy, and if you would rather be with someone else instead of me, then I want that for you too. Yes, I will be sad, but I also know that something good will come of this because that is the power of unconditional love." We remember watching him as he walked through the fire of this profoundly difficult process, and we are happy to report that he now says in hindsight that taking that approach was one of the best decisions he ever made.

Lastly, we want to remind you of this perennial truth: when one relationship ends, it creates room for another to begin. You are never too old, or too damaged, or too fill-in-the-blank to experience love at the deepest level. Your mind may tell you these things from time to time, but this is the voice of the judge and the victim, not the voice of truth. At the same time, the most important relationship you will ever have is the one you have with yourself. You are the only person with whom you will spend your entire life, so if you don't bring unconditional love to your body, mind, and spirit, it can make for an unpleasant existence. This is true whether you have a partner or not.

Explorations

Spotting and Releasing Your Anchors

There are lots of signals that you have dropped anchors, preventing your relationship vessel from sailing freely with the winds of change. Review the following list and keep it handy so that when one of these situations arises, you will know it's time to return to one of the seven secret lessons.

Frequent or unresolved fights. If you are experiencing this in your relationship, bring increased awareness and vulnerability. Frequent and unresolved fights indicate that a larger issue is lurking under the waterline. Get still and look within so that you can identify the cause. Sometimes we know what it is and we are afraid to address it. Sometimes our fear prevents us from voicing our truth, even to ourselves. Here is where you will want to find the courage to approach yourself and your partner with vulnerability. Remember, our goal is to identify what is in the shadow, face any fears associated with it, and bring it to the light in order to finally release it.

Withdrawal by one or both people. If one or both parties withdraw from engagement (and not for the purpose of cooling off with the intent to return), this can mean this person is "giving up" on a particular issue or issues. While this feels like a "win" in the short run, anytime either party withdraws and doesn't feel heard or acknowledged by the other one it's a long-term loss for the relationship as a whole. If you notice yourself withdrawing, it's time to dig deep and go back to your partner to let them know. If you feel your partner withdrawing, approach them with humility and compassion and ask them to share with you how they are feeling. This is where the practices of listening and silence in your communication are important, even when you can't find agreement on a particular issue.

Taking your partner for granted. This feeling can sneak up on us in any relationship, and it can make you or your partner feel very unappreciated. For this reason, we want to again recommend the appreciation exercise from the lesson on freedom (chapter two), as it is one of the most powerful exercises in this book. The practice of presence will aid in this as well, as nothing connects you and your partner more than just being together without the distractions of work, phones or internet, other people, or anything else that can take you mentally away from one another. When partners connect in silent presence, neither feels taken for granted.

Criticizing or blaming your partner. Minor criticisms or casting blame on your partner, either out loud or in your own mind, can provide a cue to look within and find out what you aren't accepting about yourself, your partner, or some aspect of your relationship together. When you find yourself in the midst of criticism or blame, recall the teaching "my partner is my mirror," as whatever you are attributing to your partner is often in you too. Look into your shadow and locate the conditions you have placed on your happiness, for this is the first step to releasing them.

Defensiveness. If you find yourself being defensive about something your partner says about your behavior, it often means there is some portion of truth in what they are saying. Rather than react defensively, try to lean into what they are saying and find how and in what way it could apply, even if that's not to the extent they suggest.

Seeking Professional Guidance

We are often asked about seeing a professional counselor when it comes to relationship issues. While the decision as to whether this is helpful or necessary remains up to each individual couple, we would like to share some guidelines for choosing a helping professional if you go this route. Please remember that neither of us are professional counselors, so we speak here from our own experience and that of our students.

Mutual agreement on the counselor to see. Be sure to choose someone with whom you both feel comfortable speaking. We suggest that when scheduling the first session you and your partner agree, and tell the counselor, that this visit is to see if the counselor is a good fit for you both. Let the counselor know that the two of you will discuss this after the session is over and let them know if you want to continue. Remember, if either you or your partner doesn't feel comfortable with that particular professional, we suggest meeting with someone else. It may take two or three attempts for you to find someone, but allowing time for this process early on will provide the most lasting benefit.

An agreement that the professional only sees you together. While there are different schools of thought on this, we feel that it's important that the person you choose only sees you both and does not become a primary counselor for either you or your partner as well, as this may remove this person's ability to be neutral. Should you or your partner feel you also need individual counseling in addition to couples counseling, we think it best you see another therapist so that the person you see together can maintain that separation.

Everyone has their own answers. Finally, and most importantly, we feel that you, your partner, and every human on this planet has their own answers inside themselves already. Sometimes, of course, we get lost or have trouble seeing the wisdom within, and the role of a good counselor is to help you find what is true for you. Be wary of any voice that says, "you must do this" or "you can't do that."

Please remember that this final point most certainly holds true for the information we have offered here as well. We have endeavored to share our experience in an effort to help you on the road to creating happy and healthy relationships. But remember, you and your partner's journey will be unique, and there are no "musts" here. Some of the lessons will appeal to you more than others, and that is perfectly normal. As we like to say, "take what you need and leave the rest."

Afterword

Our Wish for You

As we come to the end of this book, we want to congratulate you on the brave journey you have chosen. It takes great courage to enter into an intimate relationship, and your willingness to learn and implement these lessons in your life shows that your heart wants what is best for you and your partner.

Every spiritual tradition on this planet recognizes that relationships are a path of transformation. Being in an intimate partnership with another human creates trials and offers gifts that you would never experience living alone in a monastery or ashram. It invites you in thousands of ways to release your demands, desires, and fears over the course of your time together with your partner. As the playwright Tony Kushner says, the union of love is "the conjoining of systems in which neither loses its single splendor and both are completely transformed."

Best of all, when unconditional love is created and expressed in partnership with another, something new and beautiful is brought into the world. We are all artists, and this is an essential part of our art—the creation of a new thing that is neither of us, and both of us, and glorious.

A dear friend of ours, Addie, describes it this way:

> Here we are, 19 years deep. We love to our marrow, beyond language. Through cycles of loss and scarcity, of joy and adventure, we have learned that nothing and no one is perfect. We will hurt, we will fail, and we will succumb to fear. We commit, daily, to showing up anyway. We cultivate gratitude and full-bodied listening. We dedicate ourselves to the creation of the new in our lives and our love for one another. We seek to hold the newness lightly, so that it may grow. We search for each other in all things, and we seek to know ourselves better in our beautiful reflections.

Our hopes and wishes for you are that you will experience the same fulfillment in your relationship as our friend described—but more than that, our wish for you is that you will take the lessons presented here and use them as a guide. One of the tenets of the Toltec tradition that we practice is that the greatest wisdom in the universe is already contained within each and every one of us. While you may feel lost or clouded or unable to access those lessons, they are still inside of you.

While we have called these lessons "secrets," we want to say once again that there is nothing secret about them. The wisdom and truth of each of them exist inside us all, as we are One Life and interconnected in our energy and our shared, universal wisdom. Our intention isn't to reveal a "secret" that you would never have discovered on your own, but to provide a guide, a map, a North Star to help you find your way back to the wisdom that is within you.

In the end, you are the captain of your ship, and while you may run into choppy seas, it's your experience, your wisdom, your know-how and willingness to be open to new ideas, creative solutions, and help from your cocaptain that will allow you to traverse waves and storms without capsizing. As you dedicate yourself to this journey with your partner, also remember to dedicate yourself to *yourself* as well.

Your agreement to commit to this relationship with yourself and also your partner is what will enable you to cocreate a healthy, happy relationship.

Together.

Acknowledgments

Miguel

I want to first honor my Ink Sister, my dear friend and teaching partner, HeatherAsh Amara. Thank you for being you, and for cocreating this wonderful book with me. Your internal sun shines so bright, helping so many with your words, and I am honored to be your Ink Brother. High Five!

I also want to honor my Ink Brother, publisher, and editor, Randy Davila, and his wonderful wife, Rachel. Thank you, brother, for helping us realize our dream, and for bringing two voices together as one. Thank you Rachel, as your love for Randy and your willingness to process this book with him has helped give this book its heart.

I want to honor my Lovey, my wife and best friend, Susan Ruiz. These last fifteen years have been a wonderful journey of love, and I've learned so much from you. I can't thank you enough for being the heart of my family. It feels like home every time we are in each other's arms. I love you!

I want to honor my dear friend, my teacher and work partner, Kristie Macris. You've helped me translate my words into a language that others can understand. I want to honor those who participated in our workshops from which this book was created; your input and willingness to share with us gave this book its depth and relevancy.

Finally, I want to honor all the Angels whom I have loved. From the sweet memories of love to the bitterness of heartbreak, my heart and soul are blessed by the experience of loving you. Thank you!

HeatherAsh

To all the women and men I've loved fiercely in my lifetime; to the ones who love me still and the ones who broke my heart; to those I am no longer in touch with and those now my best friends. I am so immensely grateful for every experience, for the challenges and the beauty. Thank you for teaching me how to communicate, how to love unconditionally, how to be myself, how to stand in the fire of intimacy and be transformed by the heat. Please imagine me looking deep into your eyes, squeezing your hands, and saying, "Thank you. I love you." Feel my heart as I wrap you in a huge hug of gratitude for the gifts you brought me. You are in my heart, now and forever.

To all my students, past and present, a deep bow for being on this journey with me. You constantly teach and inspire and open me to new possibilities.

To my beloved friend and brother-in-words, don Miguel Jr., and our publisher and word-wrangler Randy, two amazing men I'm so honored to have crafted this book on relationships with. You are both bright stars in my life, thank you for your love, support, and creativity in bringing out the best in all of us to share this important message about healing and celebrating our intimate relationships.

And to you, dearest reader and seeker. May you find the healing, grace, compassion, wisdom, and courage to be vulnerable with your truth and your boundaries. May you feel held and supported as you learn to love yourself, and your beloveds, unconditionally. Keep loving, learning, playing, and remember, practice, practice, practice!

About the Authors

DON MIGUEL RUIZ JR. is a Nagual, a Toltec Master of Transformation and the author of numerous books. By combining the wisdom of his family's traditions with the knowledge gained from his own personal journey, he now helps others realize their own path to personal freedom. Please visit him at www.miguelruizjr.com.

Raised in Southeast Asia, HEATHERASH AMARA brings an openhearted, inclusive worldview to her writings and teachings. She is the author of *Warrior Goddess Training*, *The Warrior Goddess Way*, and numerous other books. Visit her online at www.heatherashamara.com.

Hierophant Publishing
8301 Broadway, Suite 219
San Antonio, TX 78209
888-800-4240

www.hierophantpublishing.com

Also by Don Miguel Ruiz Jr.

Available wherever books are sold.

Also by HeatherAsh Amara

Available wherever books are sold.